Praise for *Meeting Jesus Again for the First Time*

"In every generation there is a handful of writers of whom it can be said, 'Read everything they write.' Marcus Borg is one of these today: a writer of rare lucidity, original scholarly insights, profound spirituality, and the unusual capacity to connect it all to life in the present. He might just change your mind—or life."

Walter Wink, Auburn Theological Seminary

"It is impossible to read this beautifully written book and remain unenlightened by the results of Jesus research, or untouched by the power of Jesus' way."

Elizabeth A. Johnson, author of *She Who Is*

"For many contemporary Christians, biblical scholarship is seen as the enemy of faith. In a personal and highly readable account, Marcus Borg shows how Christians can explore contemporary scholarship as a way toward a far more dynamic and meaningful faith."

Rosemary Radford Ruether, author of *Gaia and God*

"Borg liberates 'Jesus' from the rigidity of fundamentalism and the aridity of intellectualism. He also graciously liberates readers from the shackles of what many have thought they were *supposed* to believe about Jesus if they were to remain Christians. . . . What a relief to see Jesus in a totally new light."

Alan Jones, dean, Grace Cathedral

"Marcus Borg takes his readers on a demanding and exciting tour of the New Testament. He breaks open the religious encrustations of the ages and invites us to look with fresh eyes at the Jesus that the church has distorted in the service of its doctrine and its creeds. In the process, Jesus comes to life in a startling new resurrection. I loved the book."

Rt. Rev. John Shelby Spong, Bishop of Newark;
author of *Born of a Woman*

"Just the sort of book on Jesus that we really need—a classy wedding of first-rate biblical research and solid spirituality . . . a pleasure to read."

Sandra M. Schneiders, Graduate Theological Union;
author of *The Revelatory Text*

"A book of rare excellence."

L. William Countryman, The Church Divinity School of the Pacific

Meeting Jesus AGAIN
for the First Time

THE HISTORICAL JESUS & THE
HEART OF CONTEMPORARY FAITH

Marcus J. Borg

 HarperSanFrancisco
A Division of HarperCollins*Publishers*

FIRST HARPERCOLLINS PAPERBACK EDITION PUBLISHED IN 1995

Library of Congress Cataloging-in-Publication Data

Borg, Marcus J.
    Meeting Jesus again for the first time : the historical Jesus &
    the heart of contemporary faith / Marcus J. Borg.
        p. cm.
    Includes bibliographical references and index.
    ISBN 0–06–060916–8 (cloth: alk. paper)
    ISBN 0–06–060917–6 (pbk.: alk. paper)
        1. Jesus Christ—Historicity. 2. Jesus Christ—Person and offices. I. Title.
BT303.2.B59 1994
232.9'08—dc20   93–25390
                                                                                      CIP

07 RRD(H) 40

Contents

Preface

This book owes its title—*Meeting Jesus Again for the First Time*—and much of its content to a series of lectures I delivered at the annual meeting of the Northern California Conference of the United Church of Christ at Asilomar, California, in May 1992.

The title for the lectures was given to me by John Brooke, moderator of the Northern California Conference and chair of the Asilomar meeting. Normally I provide the title for my lectures, but not in this case. I grew to like it very much. As I explain in greater detail in the first chapter, though we have all met Jesus before, meeting Jesus again can be like meeting somebody new.

In content, the book is not an exact transcript of the Asilomar lectures but has approximately doubled in size. Some features of the lecture style remain. I have permitted myself frequent use of first-person pronouns, illustrations, anecdotes, and personal references.

Occasions such as the Asilomar conference enable me to bring together the two worlds in which I live. On the one hand, I live in the world of the secular academy: as a professor at a state university, my teaching position is supported by public funds; as a Jesus scholar, the professional organizations to which I belong are committed to the nonsectarian study of Jesus and his world. In those settings, it is inappropriate to speak of the potential meanings of this material for the Christian life.

I live in a second world as well—the world of the church. I grew up in the church and have lived within it all my life, except for a hiatus of about ten years spent in a kind of exile. Since that period, which ended about a decade ago, I have not only returned to the church but become increasingly more involved in its worship and life, and more deeply committed to the Christian journey. Indeed, I am a clergy spouse: my wife, Marianne, is an Episcopal priest. I must admit that being married to a priest was not one of my childhood fantasies.

Thus I am both a secular Jesus scholar and a Christian. The Asilomar lectures (and this book) flowed out of bringing these two worlds together. This book is the product of thinking and talking about Jesus in the secular contexts of a state university and the professional academy, and of thinking and talking about Jesus in the Christian context of the church and my own life journey.

In most of my published work thus far, I have written from the scholarly place within myself. In this book, I have given myself permission to write as a Christian, even as I also write as a scholar. Thus I will seek to speak directly and unabashedly about some of the implications that, it seems to me, this material has for the Christian life.

In addition to being indebted to John Brooke for the title, I am also grateful to Francis Geddes, a United Church of Christ pastor in Fairfax, California, who was largely responsible for my invitation to deliver the lectures at Asilomar. Francis also invited me to give a series of talks titled "Jesus as Spiritual Mentor" at a week-long retreat sponsored by the Pacific Center for Spiritual Formation at Wellspring Renewal Center in Mendocino County, California, in June 1992. This book has been influenced by the experience of sharing that week with people intentionally committed to life in the Spirit.

Though this book had its immediate origin in the Asilomar conference and the Wellspring talks, it is also the evolving product of other lectures I have given in church settings, including the Palmer Lectures at the University of Puget Sound in 1989, the Bible and the Church Lectures at Christ Church Episcopal Cathedral in Indianapolis in 1991, and lecture series given in numerous local churches and to clergy groups (Presbyterian, United Church of Christ, Methodist, Lutheran, Unitarian, Metropolitan Community Church, Episcopalian, and Roman Catholic) in Oregon, Washington, Idaho, Montana, and the San Francisco Bay Area. I thank all of these groups for providing me with occasions to think and talk about the significance of Jesus for the Christian life. Finally, I wish to thank Mr. Al Hundere of San Antonio, Texas, for his generous support of my work.

Meeting Jesus Again

We have all met Jesus before. Most of us first met him when we were children. This is most obviously true for those of us raised in the church, but also for anybody who grew up in Western culture. We all received some impression of Jesus, some image of him, however vague or specific.

For many, the childhood image of Jesus remains intact into adulthood. For some, that image is held with deep conviction, sometimes linked with warm personal devotion and sometimes tied to rigid doctrinal positions. For others, both within and outside of the church, the childhood image of Jesus can become a problem, producing perplexity and doubt, often leading to indifference toward or rejection of the religion of their childhood.

Indeed, for many Christians, especially in mainline churches, there came a time when their childhood image of Jesus no longer made a great deal of sense. And for many of them, no persuasive alternative has replaced it. It is for these people especially that this book is written. For them, meeting Jesus again will be—as it has been for me—like meeting him for the first time. It will involve a new image of Jesus.

IMAGES OF JESUS
AND IMAGES OF THE CHRISTIAN LIFE

Images of Jesus matter. The foundational claim of this book is that there is a strong connection between images of Jesus and images of the Christian life, between how we think of Jesus and how we think of the Christian life. Our image of Jesus affects our perception of the Christian life in two ways: it gives shape to the Christian life; and (as we shall see later in this chapter) it can make Christianity credible or incredible.

The way images of Jesus give shape to the Christian life is illustrated by two widespread images and their effects on images of the Christian life. The most common image of Jesus—what I call the "popular image"—sees him as the divine savior. Put most compactly, this image is a constellation of answers to the three classic questions about Jesus. Who was he? The divinely begotten Son of God. What was his mission or purpose? To die for the sins of the world. What was his message? Most centrally, it was about himself: his own identity as the Son of God, the saving purpose of his death, and the importance of believing in him.

The image of the Christian life to which this image of Jesus leads is clear: it consists primarily of *believing*—that Jesus was who he said he was and that he died for our sins. We may call this a *fideistic* image of the Christian life, one whose primary dynamic is faith, understood as believing certain things about Jesus to be true. Though belief may (and ideally does) lead to much else, it is the primary quality of this image of the Christian life.

Only slightly less common is an image of Jesus as *teacher*. A de-dogmatized image of Jesus, it is held by those who are not sure what to make of the doctrinal claims made about Jesus by the Christian tradition. When these are set aside, what remains is Jesus as a great teacher. His moral teaching may be understood in quite general terms (the Great Commandment of love of God and love of neighbor, or the Golden Rule of doing to others as you would have them do to you), or in quite specific terms as a fairly narrow code of righteousness. But in either case, the image of the Christian life that flows out of this image of Jesus consists of "being good," of seeking to live as Jesus said we should.

Just as the first image of Jesus leads to a *fideistic* image of the Christian life, so this image leads to a *moralistic* image of the Christian life. Both images, it seems to me, are inadequate. Not only are they inaccurate as images of the historical Jesus, as we shall see, but they lead to incomplete images of the Christian life. That life is ultimately not about believing or about being good.

Rather, as I shall claim, it is about a relationship with God that involves us in a journey of transformation.

The understanding of the Christian life as a journey of transformation is grounded in the alternative image of Jesus that I develop in this book. This image flows out of contemporary biblical and historical scholarship. Though it may seem fresh and initially unfamiliar, it is very old, going back to the first century of the early Christian movement. Meeting this Jesus will, for many of us, be like meeting Jesus again for the first time.

MEETING JESUS AGAIN: MY OWN STORY

To recall the ways in which we have met Jesus before is illuminating. The occasion for my first doing so came unexpectedly. About two years ago I was invited to speak to an Episcopal men's group that had been meeting weekly for over ten years. Because of the nature of the group, whose times together were marked by personal sharing, their instructions to me were twofold: "Talk to us about Jesus, *and make it personal.*"

Nobody had ever asked me to do that before. I had given hundreds of lectures about Jesus, but nobody had ever said, "Make it personal." It was a challenge. Not being sure how to proceed, I wrote the words *Me and Jesus* on a piece of paper, began to think about them, and was led into memories and reflections about Jesus in my own life. It was a rich and illuminating experience, and I encourage you to try this yourself sometime. Simply begin, as I did, with your earliest childhood memories of Jesus, track them through adolescence and into adulthood, and then see what has happened to your image of Jesus over the years.

Childhood

I grew up in a small town in North Dakota near the Canadian border in the 1940s, in a world that now seems very far away. We were a Scandinavian Lutheran family, and church was important to us. Not only did I have several uncles who were Lutheran pastors, but the local Lutheran church was the center of our social life: Sunday-morning services and Sunday school, Ladies' Aid meetings that I attended with my mom, frequent church suppers, midweek services during Lent, missionary conferences, and youth groups with names like "Lutheran Children of the Reformation."

My early memories of Jesus are quite scattered. I remember pictures of Jesus with sheep, and with children. I knew he liked children; that was a big message when we were kids. Clearly, he was important. I knew that he was God's son, and that he had been born in a miraculous way. Indeed, I knew that he was "born of the virgin Mary" before I knew what a virgin was. My father's voice reading the birth story from Luke's gospel to my family as we sat around the Christmas tree on Christmas Eve comes back to me still: "And it came to pass in those days that there went out a decree from Caesar Augustus that all the world should be taxed."[1]

I also knew that Jesus died on a cross and then rose from the dead, and that all of this was very important. Easter mornings ranked second only to Christmas as festive times of the year. I knew you could pray to Jesus and even ask him to be present: "Come, Lord Jesus, be our guest" was our daily table grace. As a preschooler I memorized John 3.16 for a Sunday-school Christmas program:

> For God so loved the world that he gave his only begotten son that whosoever believes in him should not perish but have everlasting life.

The verse seemed impossibly long at the time.

And then, as the hymns of my childhood began to come back, the memories became more emotionally charged. Recalling their melodies and words moved me greatly as I sat at my desk with the words *Me and Jesus* staring up at me. As I began to say the words out loud, I found that I could not do so without my voice breaking.

Three hymns in particular came back as favorites from those early years. The first we sang often in youth group as well as in church services:

Jesus, priceless treasure, source of purest pleasure, dearest friend
    to me.
Ah, how long I've panted, and my heart hath fainted, thirsting,
    Lord, for Thee.
Thine I am, O spotless lamb; I will suffer nought to hide Thee,
Nought I ask besides Thee.

In like manner a second combined praise and devotion:

Beautiful Savior, King of Creation,
Son of God and Son of man!
Truly I'd love Thee, truly I'd serve Thee,
Light of my soul, my joy, my crown.

The third is associated with a particular memory, a missionary conference at a rural Lutheran church a few miles from our
town church. I was probably about six. It was a warm Sunday
afternoon in June, and I can remember playing with the
unfamiliar country kids in the churchyard before the service
began. The speakers were a missionary couple from China. I do
not remember what they said, but I'm sure they spoke about the
importance and challenges of the mission field. Then we sang
that great Christian missionary hymn "O Zion, Haste, Thy Mission High Fulfilling." I can vividly remember sitting next to my
parents in that white frame country church, my body still warm
and sweaty from play, and how the sunlight looked as the sanc-
tuary filled with the sound of our voices:

O Zion, haste, thy mission high fulfilling,
To tell to all the world that God is light;
That He who made all nations is not willing,
One soul should perish, lost in shades of night.
Publish glad tidings, tidings of peace,
Tidings of Jesus, redemption and release.

It was clear to me in that moment that believing in Jesus, and telling others of the tidings of Jesus, were the most important things
in the world. What was at stake was nothing less than souls
perishing, lost in shades of night.

It is tempting to see the course of my life ever since as a living out of the messages of those hymns. After all, my whole adult working life, now approaching three decades, has been spent in the scholarly study of Jesus. As my wife says about me, "He's been looking for Jesus all his life."

By the end of childhood, the ingredients of the popular image of Jesus were in place: Jesus was the divinely begotten Son of God who died for the sins of the world and whose message was about himself and his saving purpose and the importance of believing in him. Indeed, John 3.16, that verse I memorized as a preschooler, expressed this childhood image perfectly: Jesus is the divine savior in whom one is to believe for the sake of receiving eternal life.

I believed in that Jesus without difficulty and without effort. I now understand why it was so easy: I received this image of Jesus in what I have since learned to call the state of *precritical naiveté*— that childhood state in which we take for granted that whatever the significant authority figures in our lives tell us to be true is indeed true.[2] But this state of childhood belief was not to last.

The problems began not with Jesus, but with God. Sometime in elementary school, my first theological conundrum occurred. I remember being puzzled about how to put together two different things I had heard about God: that God was "everywhere present," and that God was "up in heaven." Without realizing it, I was wrestling with the relationship between the omnipresence and transcendence of God.

How could this be? I wondered. My young mind resolved the puzzle in favor of God up in heaven. The omnipresence of God, I decided, meant that God *could* be anywhere God decided to be. God *could* even appear right in this room right now. But of course, most of the time God is not here; rather, God is up in heaven. Unwittingly, my resolution of the perplexity reduced God's omnipresence to a magical potentiality to be anywhere.

Also unwittingly, I had taken the first step in removing God from the world. The solution I arrived at indicated that I had come to think of God as a supernatural being "out there." God became distant and remote, far away and removed from the world, except for special interventions, such as the ones described in the Bible. But I still had no doubts that God was real. Those were to begin later.

Adolescence

In my early teens, I began to have doubts about the existence of God. It was an experience filled with anxiety, guilt, and fear. I still believed enough to be afraid of going to hell because of my doubts. I felt that they were wrong, and in my prayers I would ask for forgiveness. But I couldn't stop doubting, and so my requests for forgiveness seemed to me not to be genuine. After all, I had learned that true repentance included the resolution not to continue committing the sin.

Every night for several years, I prayed with considerable anguish, "Lord, I believe. Help thou my unbelief." The inability to overcome my doubt confirmed for me that I had become more of an unbeliever than a believer. In retrospect, I can also see that, for me at least, belief is not a matter of the will. I desperately wanted to believe and to be delivered from the anguish I was experiencing. If I could have made myself believe, I would have.

Unlike my earlier perplexity about God's "everywhere-ness," my doubt about God's existence was not connected to any particular element in my belief system, but concerned the foundation of the system itself. I now understand what was happening: I was experiencing a collision between the modern worldview and my childhood beliefs. The modern worldview, with its image of what is real as the world of matter and energy and its vision of the universe as a closed system of cause and effect, made belief in God—a nonmaterial reality—increasingly problematic. I had entered the stage of critical thinking, and there was no way back.

And, of course, these doubts about God affected how I thought of Jesus. What does it mean to speak of Jesus as the Son of God when one is no longer sure that God is?

College

As adolescence ended, I went off to a Lutheran college in the Midwest with a conventional but no longer deeply held understanding of the Christian faith. The nightly prayers for belief stopped. Apparently I no longer believed enough to be frightened of hell. The fear and guilt had been reduced to a perplexity that I would occasionally, but not often, think about. Other matters caught my attention.

Then in my junior year, in a required religion course, I was exposed to the scholarly study of theology by a brilliant young professor with a fresh Ph.D. from the University of Chicago.[3] Intellectually, it was the most exciting material I had ever encountered. The course covered all the big questions: God, the nature of reality, human nature, evil, atonement, ethics, the relationship between Christianity and other religions, and so forth. It exposed me to the diversity of answers provided by the intellectual giants of the tradition, ancient and modern: Augustine, Aquinas, Anselm, Schleiermacher, Barth, Bultmann, Tillich, Eliade, and so on. The experience was fascinating and liberating. Its effect on me was that the sacred cows of inherited belief began to fall in a way that legitimated their demise. But it didn't help me to believe. Rather, it provided a framework within which I could take my perplexity seriously.

Judging from later conversations with many Christians, I think my journey as described thus far is fairly typical. As college ended, the images of Christianity and of Jesus that I had received as a child were no longer persuasive or compelling. I had become aware that it was difficult and perhaps not necessary to take the Bible and Christian teachings literally, but I didn't know what a nonliteral approach might mean. My childhood understanding of Christianity had collapsed, but nothing had replaced it. I had become a "closet agnostic," someone who didn't know what to make of it all.

Seminary and Beyond

And so I went off to seminary. That didn't help. To put it more precisely, that didn't help the faith dimension of my journey, which was still years away from resolution. But seminary was tremendously illuminating; the insights flowing from theological education are immensely helpful in sorting out what it means to take the Christian life seriously.

Jesus once again moved center stage. This happened because of my first-semester New Testament course.[4] There I learned that the image of Jesus from my childhood—the popular image of Jesus as the divine savior who knew himself to be the Son of God and who offered up his life for the sins of the world—was not historically true. That, I learned, was not what the historical Jesus was like.

The basis for this mind-boggling realization was the understanding of the gospels that has developed over the last two hundred years of biblical scholarship. I learned that the gospels are neither divine documents nor straightforward historical records. They are not divine products inspired directly by God, whose contents therefore are to be believed (as I had thought prior to this). Nor are they eyewitness accounts written by people who had accompanied Jesus and simply sought to report what they had seen and heard.

Rather, I learned, the gospels represent the developing traditions of the early Christian movement. Written in the last third of the first century, they contain the accumulated traditions of early Christian communities and were put into their present forms by second- (or even third-) generation authors.[5] Through careful comparative study of the gospels, one can see these authors at work, modifying and adding to the traditions they received.[6] They were continuing a process that had been going on throughout the forty to seventy years when the gospel material circulated in oral form. Much happened in those decades to change the traditions about Jesus.

It is not so much that memories grew dim, or that the oral tradition was unreliable. Rather, two primary factors were at work. First, the traditions about Jesus were adapted and applied to the changing circumstances of the early Christian movement. Jesus himself spoke in a Palestinian Jewish milieu. The gospels were written in and for communities that had begun to move beyond Palestine and into the larger Mediterranean world, and the gospel writers adapted the materials about Jesus to these new settings. Second, the movement's beliefs about Jesus *grew* during those decades. We can see that growth by arranging the gospel material chronologically, from earlier to later writings. As the decades passed, the early Christian movement increasingly spoke of Jesus as divine and as having the qualities of God, a development that within a few centuries was to result in the doctrine of the Trinity.

The gospels are the products of communities experiencing these developments. As such, they contain not only the movement's memories of the historical Jesus, but those memories added to and modified by the growing beliefs and changing circumstances of the movement. Thus the gospels are the church's memories of the historical Jesus transformed by the community's experience and reflection in the decades after Easter. They therefore tell us what these early Christian communities had come to believe about Jesus by the last third of the first century. They are not, first and foremost, reports of the ministry itself.

This understanding of the gospels is the basis for the well-known scholarly distinction between *the Jesus of history* and *the Christ of faith*, which I also learned about in that first seminary course. The first phrase refers to Jesus as the particular person he was—Jesus of Nazareth, a Galilean Jew of the first century who was executed by the Romans. The second phrase refers to the Christ of the developing Christian tradition—namely, what Jesus became in the faith of the early Christian communities in the decades after his death.

It is the Christ of faith whom we encounter on the surface level of the gospels, as well as in the fully developed Christian creeds of the fourth and fifth centuries. That Jesus—the Christ of faith—is spoken of as divine, indeed coequal with God, of one substance with God, begotten before all worlds, the second person of the Trinity. I learned that Jesus as a human being—the historical Jesus—was quite different from all of that. For one thing, he would not have known any of those things about himself.

This was news. Before becoming aware of all of this, I had quite unreflectively combined what I heard about the Christ of faith with my image of Jesus as a historical figure. Though of course I had been aware that Jesus had lived a human life, I had also assumed that even as a human being he was the second person of the Trinity and would have known that about himself. Now, along with learning about the nature of the gospels as the developing tradition of the church, I learned that there was sharp discontinuity (rather than continuity) between the historical Jesus and the Christ of Christian tradition.

The understanding of John's gospel that emerged in that first seminary course provides a good way of illustrating the combined effects of this new knowledge. The picture of Jesus in John is clearly quite different from the picture of Jesus in Matthew, Mark, and Luke, which are collectively known as the synoptic gospels.

In John, Jesus speaks as a divine person. The great "I am" statements ("I am the bread of life," "the light of the world," "the vine, the way, the truth and the life," and so on) are all peculiar to John. So are statements such as "I and the Father are one" and "He who has seen me has seen the Father." In the synoptic gospels, Jesus speaks very differently; his message is not about himself or his identity. Like most Christians, I had simply harmonized these two different images, and indeed had not really been aware of how different they are. I had assumed that Jesus talked both as he does in John and as he does in the synoptic gospels.

Now I learned (and saw for myself) a different explanation. The contrast between the synoptic and Johannine images of Jesus is so great that one of them must be nonhistorical. Both cannot be accurate characterizations of Jesus as a historical figure. The verdict of nonhistorical went to John. I learned that the portrait of Jesus in John's gospel was essentially one of the Christ of faith, and not the Jesus of history. Jesus never spoke of himself as the Son of God, as one with God, as the light of the world, as the way, the truth, and the life, and so forth. Indeed, he never spoke the words of John 3.16—that verse from my childhood that had summed up my image of Jesus.

I am aware that this is still news for some Christians, even though it has been old hat in the seminaries of mainline denominations throughout this century. It was news to me when I heard it, and its effect on my image of Jesus as divine savior—the popular image—was dramatic. I saw that this image was basically drawn from the later portions of the gospel tradition—largely from John's gospel, supplemented by the birth stories in Matthew and Luke. Indeed, the linkage between John's gospel and the popular image of Jesus was so strong that I remember becoming angry at John when I first became aware that its account was largely nonhistorical. I saw John as containing a distorted image of Jesus, an image I had spent years trying to believe in. I would have been happy to have John excised from the New Testament.

(I now see John very differently, and will say more about that shortly.)

Thus the cumulative effect of my first seminary New Testament course upon my image of Jesus was staggering. In addition, I learned of two further consensus positions then dominant in Jesus scholarship. The first was that we can't know very much at all about the Jesus of history. Not only was John's gospel seen as nonhistorical, but it was felt that even within the synoptic gospels it was very difficult to discern the voice of Jesus from the voice of the church. Midcentury Jesus scholarship was marked by thoroughgoing skepticism, coupled with the claim that only the Christ of faith is theologically significant.

The second consensus position concerned what little we could know about Jesus—namely, that he was an "eschatological prophet" who expected and proclaimed the end of the present world and the coming of the Kingdom of God in the very near future. That (and not his own identity or the importance of believing in him) was the content of his message and the basis of his urgent call to repent: the world was soon to pass away; therefore, ground yourself in God. About the nearness of the end he was, of course, wrong.

I must admit that it was not a very satisfying image of Jesus. Yet it was the image that a generation or two of seminary students received: we can't know much about Jesus, and what we can know is that he was wrong about the central conviction animating his ministry and message, and in any case it doesn't really matter, for the historical Jesus is theologically irrelevant.

As a twenty-two-year-old seminarian, I found all of this very exciting, though it also seemed vaguely scandalous and something I shouldn't tell my mother about. The news that Jesus was very different from what we think he was like seemed an important piece of information. And it aroused my curiosity: if Jesus' message wasn't about himself as the Son of God whose purpose was to die for our sins, what was his message, and what was he up to?

In fact, *curiosity* is too weak a word. I had not planned to be a New Testament or Jesus scholar when I went to seminary (indeed, I had not even planned to go to seminary, but that's another story). Nevertheless, I became captivated by the question of Jesus, and have been involved in the scholarly quest for the historical Jesus ever since.

But back to seminary and the years of graduate school that followed. Even as I was becoming fascinated with the study of the Christian tradition and the quest for the historical Jesus, my unbelief was deepening. The "closet agnostic" was becoming a "closet atheist," though I never acknowledged that to anybody. The reasons are clear enough to me now. The central problem was still the collision between God and the modern worldview, between my image of God and the image of reality I had acquired by growing up in the modern world. The latter had hardened into a taken-for-granted "map" of reality. Indeed, I didn't even think of it as a map, but simply as the way things are.

Moreover, the longer I studied the Christian tradition, the more transparent its human origins became. Religions in general (including Christianity), it seemed to me, were manifestly cultural products. I could see how their readily identifiable psychological and social functions served human needs and cultural ends. The notion that we made it all up was somewhat alarming, but also increasingly compelling.

And so, though I found the study of the Bible and the Christian tradition to be immensely rich and rewarding, the bottom line was that in the end I didn't know what to do with the notion of God. On the whole, I thought that there probably was no such reality.

This uncertainty about God affected the focus of my research on Jesus. For about the first dozen years, I concentrated on what we can glimpse about Jesus' relationship to "this world." I focused on his involvement with the social and political issues of his day, especially his challenge to the purity system of the first-century Jewish social world.[7] I argued that he was an advocate of the politics of compassion in a social world dominated by the politics of purity (about which I shall say more in a later chapter). In short, I studied those parts of the tradition that made sense apart from the God question. But even as I did this, I remained aware that Jesus was more than a sociopolitical figure, although I didn't know what to make of what he said about God.

Then in my mid-thirties I had a number of experiences of what I now recognize as "nature mysticism." In a sense, they were nothing spectacular, at least not compared with the experiences described by William James in his classic work *The Varieties of Religious Experience.*[8] But they fundamentally changed my understanding of God, Jesus, religion, and Christianity.

The experiences were marked by what the Jewish theologian Abraham Heschel called "radical amazement," moments of transformed perception in which the earth is seen as "filled with the glory of God," shining with a radiant presence.[9] They were also moments of connectedness in which I felt my linkage to what is.

They seemed similar to the experiences that Rudolf Otto described as experiences of the "numinous," the awe-inspiring and wonder-evoking "holy," the *mysterium tremendum et fascinans* (the tremendous, overwhelming mystery that elicits trembling even as it also attracts us in a compelling way).[10] They involved a rediscovery of mystery—not an intellectual paradox, but an experience of sacred mystery.

These experiences, besides being ecstatic, were for me *aha!* moments. They gave me a new understanding of the meaning of the word *God.* I realized that *God* does not refer to a supernatural being "out there" (which is where I had put God ever since my childhood musings about God "up in heaven"). Rather, I began to see, the word *God* refers to the sacred at the center of existence, the holy mystery that is all around us and within us. God is the nonmaterial ground and source and presence in which, to cite words attributed to Paul by the author of Acts, "we live and move and have our being"[11]

Thus I began also to understand what it means to say that God is both everywhere present and "up in heaven"—both immanent and transcendent, as traditional Christian theology puts it. As immanent (the root means "to dwell within"), God is not somewhere else, but right here and everywhere. To speak of God as being "up in heaven"—that is, as transcendent—means that God is not to be identified with any particular thing, not even with the sum total of things.

God is more than everything, and yet everything is in God. Being a thinking type, I began studying experiences of God in both mystical and nonmystical forms. I learned that even though these experiences are extraordinary, they are also quite common, known across cultures, throughout history, and into the present time. Gradually it became obvious to me that God—the sacred, the holy, the numinous—was "real." God was no longer a concept or an article of belief, but had become an element of experience.

How I See Jesus Now

This transformation in my understanding of God began to affect my understanding of Jesus. I now was able to see the centrality of God (or "the Spirit," to say the same thing) in Jesus' own life. I began to see Jesus as one whose spirituality—his experiential awareness of Spirit—was foundational for his life. This perception became the vantage point for what I have since come to understand as the key truth about Jesus: that in addition to being deeply involved in the social world of the everyday, he was also grounded in the world of the Spirit. Indeed, as I shall observe from several perspectives in this book, Jesus' relationship to the Spirit was the source of everything that he was.

THE PRE-EASTER AND THE POST-EASTER JESUS

As I have continued my study of Jesus, the distinction between the historical Jesus and the Christ of faith that I learned about in my first seminary course remains of first importance. There simply is a major difference between what Jesus was like as a figure of history and how he is spoken of in the gospels and later Christian tradition. However, I have begun to prefer using another set of phrases to express the contrast: *the pre-Easter Jesus* and *the post-Easter Jesus.* They seem more precise and illuminating.

By *the pre-Easter Jesus,* I mean, of course, Jesus as a figure of history before his death. Most of this book concerns the pre-Easter Jesus. Moreover, I shall provide a sketch of how I see the pre-Easter Jesus in the next chapter, so I shall not say more about him now.

I have come to prefer speaking of *the post-Easter Jesus* rather than *the Christ of faith.* The latter phrase always suggested to me a rather problematic reality. The choice of words implied that the "real" Jesus was the Jesus of history, whereas the Christ of faith could only be believed in. The first could (at least in principle) be known; the second could be accepted only by faith.

For me, the phrase *the post-Easter Jesus* gets past that difficulty. I define *the post-Easter Jesus* as the Jesus of Christian tradition and *experience*. That is, the post-Easter Jesus is not just the product of early Christian belief and thought, but an element of *experience*.

Indeed, this seems to me to be the central meaning of Easter. Beginning with Easter, the early movement continued to experience Jesus as a living reality after his death, *but in a radically new way*. After Easter, his followers experienced him as a spiritual reality, no longer as a person of flesh and blood, limited in time and space, as Jesus of Nazareth had been. Rather, Jesus as the risen living Christ could be experienced anywhere and everywhere. Increasingly he was spoken of as having all of the qualities of God. Prayers were addressed to Jesus as God, and praise was offered to Jesus as God in Christian worship. In short, his early followers experienced the risen Christ and addressed the risen Christ as the functional equivalent of God, as "one with God."

So it has been ever since. The living risen Christ of the New Testament has been an experiential reality (and not just an article of belief) from the days of Easter to the present. Thus, in the experience, worship, and devotion of Christians throughout the centuries, the post-Easter Jesus is real.

This awareness has helped me to see the gospel of John in a new light. The anger I felt toward John when I first learned it was not an accurate portrayal of the historical Jesus has been replaced by a deep appreciation. To use the great "I am" statements that run throughout John to illustrate this point, why would the early Christian community out of which John's gospel comes portray Jesus as saying about himself, "I am the light of the world," "I am the bread of life," "I am the way, the truth, and the life," if Jesus did not speak that way about himself? I now see the answer: this is how they experienced the post-Easter Jesus. For them, the post-Easter Jesus was the light that led them out of darkness, the spiritual food that nourished them in the midst of their journey, the way that led them from death to life.

That is, John's gospel is a powerful testimony to the reality and significance of the post-Easter Jesus, the living Christ of Christian experience. John's gospel is "true," even though its account of Jesus' life story and sayings is not, by and large, historically factual. My journey from the childhood state of precritical naiveté through the critical thinking of adolescence and adulthood now led to hearing John (and the Bible as a whole) in a state of postcritical naiveté—a state in which one can hear these stories as "true stories," even while knowing that they are not literally true.[12]

BEYOND BELIEF TO RELATIONSHIP

Finally, as I complete my story of how I met Jesus again, I want to mention briefly how these changes in my image of Jesus affected my vision of the Christian life. Until my late thirties, I saw the Christian life as being primarily about *believing*. Like many of us, as a child I had no problem with belief. But at the end of childhood there began a period, lasting over twenty years, in which, like many, I struggled with doubt and disbelief. All through this period I continued to think that believing was what the Christian life was all about. Yet no matter how hard I tried, I was unable to "do" that, and I wondered how others could.

Now I no longer see the Christian life as being primarily about believing. The experiences of my mid-thirties led me to realize that God is and that the central issue of the Christian life is not believing in God or believing in the Bible or believing in the Christian tradition. Rather, the Christian life is about entering into a relationship with that to which the Christian tradition points, which may be spoken of as God, the risen living Christ, or the Spirit. And a Christian is one who lives out his or her relationship to God within the framework of the Christian tradition.

I sometimes joke that if I were ever to write my spiritual autobiography, I would call it "Beyond Belief." The fuller title would be "Beyond Belief to Relationship." That has been my experience. My own journey has led beyond belief (and beyond doubt and disbelief) to an understanding of the Christian life as a relationship to the Spirit of God—a relationship that involves one in a journey of transformation. It is this understanding of the Christian life that I will develop in the rest of this book.

NOTES

1. Luke 2.1, KJV (the Bible used in my childhood); the story continues through 2.20. Most often in this book I use the New Revised Standard Version as a basis for quotations from the Bible, which I have modified for greater clarity or to make pronouns for God gender inclusive. I use inclusive language not as a matter of "political correctness" but because of its intrinsic importance.

2. This notion was developed by Paul Ricoeur, who refers to precritical naiveté as "first naiveté" and to the parallel (but quite different) state of postcritical naiveté as "second naiveté" (see my discussion of this latter state later in this chapter). For an excellent study of Ricoeur's approach to Scripture, see Mark Wallace, *The Second Naiveté: Barth, Ricoeur, and the New Yale Theology* (Macon, GA: Mercer Univ. Press, 1990).

3. My teacher was Paul Sponheim, now a professor of theology at Luther Northwestern Seminary in St. Paul, Minnesota, and the author of a number of books on Christian theology.

4. The course was taught by the British scholar W. D. Davies at Union Theological Seminary in Manhattan. In the spectrum of biblical scholarship at the time, Davies was a moderate, reflecting the moderation characteristic of much British New Testament scholarship.

5. The church throughout its history has consistently referred to the authors of the gospels as *evangelists*. The term rightly suggests that they are not disinterested reporters or straightforward historians, but *proclaimers of a message:* the "good news" of the new life available through Jesus.

6. For an excellent, accessible introduction to this understanding of the gospels, see W. Barnes Tatum, *In Quest of Jesus* (Atlanta: John Knox, 1982). The most widely accepted scholarly understanding is that Mark is the earliest gospel, written around A.D. 70. Matthew and Luke were written some ten to twenty years later, and both used Mark as well as the document known as "Q," a collection of sayings of Jesus totaling about two hundred verses, perhaps collected together as early as A.D. 50. John may be independent of the other three gospels and is typically dated around A.D. 90 to 100.

7. I pursued these themes in my 1972 doctoral thesis at Oxford (supervised by George B. Caird) and in my first book about Jesus, *Conflict, Holiness and Politics in the Teachings of Jesus* (New York and Toronto: Edwin Mellen, 1984); that book is a major revision and expansion of the thesis.

8. William James, *The Varieties of Religious Experience,* ed. Martin Marty (New York: Penguin, 1982; originally published in 1902). Though almost a century old, this classic work is still a rich introduction to the varieties of firsthand religious experience.

9. Abraham Heschel, *Man Is Not Alone: A Philosophy of Religion* (New York: Farrar, Straus and Giroux, 1951).

10. Rudolf Otto, *The Idea of the Holy* (New York: Oxford Univ. Press, 1958; first published in German in 1917).

11. Acts 17.28. For another well-known biblical passage that speaks of God as the encompassing everywhere-present Spirit, see Psalm 139.

12. The state of postcritical naiveté is nicely illustrated by the account of an Native American storyteller who always began telling his tribe's story of creation by saying, "Now, I don't know if it happened this way or not, but I know this story is true."

What Manner of Man?

THE PRE-EASTER JESUS

If Jesus of Nazareth was not like the popular image of him, what was he like? Before we turn to specific themes of his message and activity in the rest of this book, I will provide a preliminary sketch of what we may surmise about him as a historical person. In this chapter, I will introduce you to the pre-Easter Jesus.

FROM THE GOSPELS TO JESUS

Before I sketch my own image of the pre-Easter Jesus, it will be helpful to consider what is involved. As I mentioned in chapter 1, the gospels are not straightforward historical documents but are the developing traditions of the early Christian movement put into written form in the last third of the first century. In the forty to seventy years between the ministry of Jesus and the writing of the gospels, the early Christians not only adapted the traditions about Jesus to new circumstances, but also continued to experience Jesus as a living reality after his death. The gospels contain both their memories of Jesus of Nazareth and their ongoing experience of the post-Easter Jesus.

There are thus minimally two layers of tradition or two kinds of material in the gospels. Some material goes back to the pre-Easter Jesus, and some is the product of the early Christian movement. To put it another way, the gospels contain minimally two voices—the voice of the pre-Easter Jesus and the voice of the community in the post-Easter setting. Constructing an image of the pre-Easter Jesus involves separating out these layers, these voices.

The work of a group of scholars known as the Jesus Seminar illustrates this process well. Since we began in 1985, we have met twice a year for the sake of voting on the historical accuracy of the sayings of Jesus. To many people, the idea of voting on Jesus seems bizarre, and, to some, blasphemous. But our voting has a simple purpose: to measure the degree of scholarly consensus on how much of this material goes back to Jesus himself. We vote on each saying by casting one of four differently colored beads into a ballot box. The different colors—red, pink, gray, and black—represent a descending spectrum of historical probability. A red vote means, "I'm pretty sure Jesus said that"; pink, somewhere between "probably" and "more likely yes than no"; gray, somewhere between "more likely no than yes" and "probably not"; and black, "I'm pretty sure Jesus didn't say that."

To relate the work of the Seminar to the understanding of the gospels as containing minimally two layers or voices: a red vote means, "This is a part of the gospel that is very close to the voice of the pre-Easter Jesus"; a pink vote means, "Yes, the voice of Jesus is still present, but it is beginning to be affected by the developing voice of the community"; a gray vote points to a saying that is even more the voice of the community; and a black vote means, "This is almost exclusively (and perhaps entirely) the voice of the community."[1]

If we separate these voices out, what image of the pre-Easter Jesus emerges? Our written sources for addressing that question are primarily twofold. The first (and most important) source is the early layers of Matthew, Mark, and Luke (the synoptic gospels, also known simply as the synoptics), which contain sayings of Jesus, typical actions, and a skeletal framework of his adult ministry. Our second source is the early layer of the recently discovered Gospel of Thomas, found in upper Egypt in 1945.

Thomas consists solely of sayings of Jesus (114 in all), and a strong case can be made that some of these go back to Jesus himself.[2]

Missing from our list of sources is the gospel of John. As I noted in chapter 1, though it is a powerful and truthful testimony to the community's experience of the post-Easter Jesus, it does not very closely reflect the pre-Easter Jesus. To use the color code of the Jesus Seminar, almost all of John has received only black votes. And so we return to our question: what was the pre-Easter Jesus like?

THE JEWISHNESS OF JESUS

Jesus was deeply Jewish. It is important to emphasize this obvious fact. Not only was he Jewish by birth and socialization, but he remained a Jew all of his life. His Scripture was the Jewish Bible. He did not intend to establish a new religion, but saw himself as having a mission within Judaism. He spoke as a Jew to other Jews. His early followers were Jewish. All of the authors of the New Testament (with the possible exception of the author of Luke-Acts) were Jewish.

Though I find it hard to believe, some Christians are apparently unaware of the Jewishness of Jesus, or, if they are aware, do not give it much weight.[3] Moreover, Christians have frequently been guilty of conscious or unconscious anti-Semitism, identifying Jesus with Christianity and his opponents with Judaism, and thereby seeing Jesus and the early Christian movement as anti-Jewish. Parts of the New Testament as well as the popular image of Jesus encourage the notion that "the Jews" rejected Jesus.

But Jesus' opponents did not represent the Jewish people or nation. "The Jews" did not reject Jesus. Rather, the few Jewish persons involved in the events leading to his execution were a small but powerful elite whose power derived from the Romans. Instead of representing the Jews, they might fairly be described as collaborating in the oppression of the Jewish people.

The separation of Jesus from Judaism has had tragic consequences for Jews throughout the centuries. The separation is also historically incorrect, and any faithful image of Jesus must take with utmost seriousness his rootedness in Judaism.

STORIES OF JESUS' BIRTH

We know very little about Jesus before the beginning of his public activity. In the opinion of most mainstream scholars, the stories of his birth and childhood are not historical. Because this is still news to many within the church, it is worthwhile describing why these stories are seen this way.

Within the New Testament, the birth of Jesus is referred to only in two relatively late sources, the gospels of Matthew and Luke, both written in the last twenty years of the first century. Paul, the earliest New Testament author, whose genuine letters were written between approximately A.D. 48 and his death sometime between A.D. 62 and 64, does not mention Jesus being born in a special way. Neither does Mark, the earliest gospel, written around the year 70. Nor does the gospel of John. At the very least, this suggests that stories about the birth of Jesus were not central to the early Christian movement.

Moreover, the stories of his birth as found in Matthew and Luke are very different from each other. The differences include the following:

In Matthew, the genealogy of Jesus goes back to Abraham, the father of the Jewish people, and from David onward is traced through the kings of Israel. In Luke, the genealogy of Jesus goes back to Adam, the father of both Jews and Gentiles, and from David onward is traced through the prophets of Israel.

In Matthew, the family of Jesus lives in Bethlehem, where Jesus is born *at home,* and moves to Nazareth after returning from the flight into Egypt. In Luke, the family of Jesus lives in Nazareth and travels to Bethlehem because of the census, and so Jesus is born "on the road" in a stable, after which the family returns to its home in Nazareth.

In Matthew, the people who come to the birth are the wise men following the star. In Luke, there is neither star nor wise men; rather, there are shepherds.

In Matthew, King Herod the Great orders the slaughter of male infants in Bethlehem, which leads Jesus' family to seek refuge in Egypt. In Luke, there is no such slaughter and no flight into Egypt.

These differences are the basis upon which most scholars conclude that the birth stories are not historical accounts but symbolic narratives created by the early Christian movement. To some extent, they reflect themes important to each evangelist. For example, with his tracing of Jesus' genealogy through the kings of Israel and with his story of the wise men seeking the one who is born "king of the Jews," Matthew emphasizes Jesus' kingship. Luke, with Jesus' genealogy traced back through the prophets, and with shepherds (who were marginalized people) as the ones to whom the news of the birth comes, emphasizes Jesus as a radical social prophet.

The birth stories make use of more primal religious imagery as well. With their stories of Jesus' conception by the Spirit, both Matthew and Luke affirm that what happened in Jesus was not simply "of the flesh," but also "of God"—that is, "of the Spirit." Both powerfully express the ancient theme of light coming into the darkness, Matthew with the star shining as a beacon to the wise men, Luke with the glory of God appearing in the night sky as the angels sing to the shepherds. The decision of the Christian church in the fourth century to celebrate Jesus' birth at the time of the winter solstice expresses this symbolism perfectly (at least in the Northern Hemisphere): he is born at the time of deepest darkness, and his birth is the coming of the light. Or, to put it even more compactly, Jesus is the light in our darkness. To hear the birth stories again in a state of postcritical naiveté is to be able to hear their rich symbolic affirmations without needing to believe them as historical reports.

Of course, these stories also say something indirectly about the historical Jesus, even though it is highly doubtful that they tell us anything about his birth. Namely, they tell us that he was such an extraordinary person that these kinds of stories were told about him. Similar stories were told about others, too. But how did it happen that such stories were told about a marginalized Jew from Galilee? The stories raise the question, What manner of man was this?

JESUS' SOCIALIZATION
AND EARLY ADULTHOOD

As we move beyond the canonical birth stories to stories that seek to fill in the missing years of Jesus, the same verdict—nonhistorical—applies. A collection of such stories is found in the late second-century Infancy Gospel of Thomas (not to be confused with the *sayings* Gospel of Thomas), which reports some quite remarkable episodes about Jesus as a boy. At around age five, for example, he makes sparrows out of clay on the sabbath and, when criticized for breaking the sabbath by "working," claps his hands and they fly away. At around age six, a playmate accidentally jostles Jesus' shoulder:

> Jesus was exasperated and said to him: "You shall not go further on your way," and the child immediately fell down and died.[4]

These fanciful tales assigning extraordinary powers to the child Jesus are the products of early Christian imagination, in which the divine status of the post-Easter Jesus is uncritically projected back earlier and earlier into his life.[5]

In short, we do not have any historically reliable stories about Jesus before about age thirty.[6] However, from the gospels a few conclusions may be derived. He was probably born very near the end of the reign of Herod the Great, and therefore shortly before 4 B.C.[7] His parents were Jewish, and their names were Mary and Joseph. He may have been the firstborn, though this is not certain. He had four brothers and an unknown number of sisters, all presumably children of Joseph and Mary. Joseph probably died before Jesus' public activity began.[8]

Jesus grew up in Nazareth, in the hill country of southern Galilee, about a hundred miles north of Jerusalem. Population estimates for Nazareth vary widely, from two hundred to two thousand people. Nazareth was less than four miles from the city of Sepphoris, whose population of forty thousand made it the largest in Galilee. Sepphoris had been destroyed by the Romans as they were quelling a rebellion that arose when Herod the Great died in 4 B.C. Rebuilt during Jesus' youth, it was quite cosmopolitan. The reconstruction included a Roman-style theater built sometime in the first century in which Greek and Roman plays were performed, though it is not clear that it can be dated as early as Jesus' lifetime. But it is rather intriguing to imagine Jesus going to the theater as a young man.

Indeed, Jesus' environment was considerably more cosmopolitan than we have typically imagined. The debate about the degree of Hellenization in Galilee continues among scholars, but it is clear that Galilee was not a bucolic rural backwater. In addition to Sepphoris, there were four other cities within about fifteen miles of Nazareth. Trade with other parts of the Mediterranean world was extensive, and foreign goods such as beer imported from Egypt were available. The area contained a considerable number of Gentiles, and the Greek language was widely used. It is possible that many or most Jews were bilingual, speaking both Aramaic and Greek. And, of course, the whole of Palestine was under Gentile control. Since 63 B.C., it had been part of the Roman Empire, ruled by "client kings" appointed by Rome.

From a few hints in the gospels and from what we might imagine about the socialization of a Jewish boy in first-century Galilee, we can surmise a few things about Jesus' youth. It is quite likely that he went to school in the synagogue in Nazareth, where the emphasis would have been on reading and writing, with the Torah as the primary text.[9] He probably became a woodworker (in Greek, *tektōn*).[10] The word *tektōn* has been translated as, but had a meaning different from, our word *carpenter*—that is, one who works on wooden buildings. For the most part, buildings were not made of wood in Palestine. Rather, a *tektōn* made wood products: doors, door frames, roof beams, furniture, cabinets, boxes, even yokes and plows. In terms of social standing, a *tektōn* was at the lower end of the peasant class, more marginalized than a peasant who still owned a small piece of land. We should not think of a *tektōn* as being a step up from a subsistence farmer; rather, a *tektōn* belonged to a family that had lost its land.

If his family was at least somewhat devout—a common assumption among Bible scholars—Jesus would have participated in the practices of "common Judaism."[11] He would have learned the stories, hymns, and prayers of the Jewish tradition. He would have observed and celebrated the great Jewish holidays, three of which were pilgrimage festivals, ideally to be spent in Jerusalem. Passover, in the spring, recalled the exodus from Egypt. Pentecost (or "the Feast of Weeks"), some fifty days later, was an agricultural festival celebrating God's ownership of the land and thanking God for its fruitfulness. Tabernacles (or "the Feast of Booths") was an eight-day harvest celebration in the fall, marked by much music, feasting, and dancing; it recalled the forty years spent in the wilderness. During this festival everybody was to live in temporary dwellings or "booths."[12] It is reasonable to think that Jesus at least occasionally went on pilgrimage to Jerusalem to observe these festivals. Though we do not know much about daily and weekly religious practices at the time of Jesus, it is probable that he, like most Jews, prayed the Shema twice daily, upon rising and going to bed.[13] He no doubt observed the sabbath, which included attending the synagogue for Torah study and prayer.

At some point in his life, Jesus must have become a religious seeker and embarked upon a religious quest. This is the most obvious explanation of one of the most certain facts we know about him: in his late twenties or around the age of thirty, he left Nazareth and became a follower of a wilderness prophet named John. We do not know whether this decision was the result of a gradual maturing or the product of a more sudden and dramatic religious experience. But something led him to leave conventional life behind and go out to the wilderness to become a follower of John the Baptizer.

We may further surmise that Jesus probably underwent what William James calls a "conversion experience." The conversion, of course, was not from paganism to Judaism, for he grew up Jewish. Rather, as James defines it, *conversion* need not refer to changing from one religion to another, or from being nonreligious to being religious; it may also refer to a process, whether sudden or gradual, whereby religious impulses and energies become central to one's life.[14] It is reasonable to suppose that Jesus experienced such an internal transformation, which led him to undertake the ministry that he did, and that this probably had something to do with John the Baptizer.

Clearly, Jesus' relationship to John was important. Not only do all the gospels begin the story of Jesus' adult activity with his association with John, but about him Jesus is reported to have said, "There is no one born of woman greater than John."[15] That is high praise. Moreover, Mark dates the beginning of Jesus' ministry to John's arrest, which suggests minimally that, with his mentor in prison, Jesus stepped in to carry on. Beyond the minimal, we may wonder if the arrest and execution of the Baptizer were even more significant for Jesus.[16] In any case, it is in connection with John that Jesus' personal story became public history.

THE ADULT JESUS: A SKETCH

So what was the adult Jesus like? What did this person, born to Mary and Joseph, socialized in Nazareth, and discipled to John the Baptizer, become?

Answering this question involves us in the task of historical reconstruction, which may be understood as generating an image or gestalt that draws together into a cohesive whole the various elements of the tradition judged to be historical. The process is very much like a particular stage of detective work: after the evidence has been gathered, analyzed, and weighed, it has to be integrated into an overall hypothesis.

Doing this with the traditions about Jesus produces a sketch, or construal or gestalt or image, of Jesus. I prefer these terms to *picture* or *portrait*, both of which suggest too much fullness of detail. A *sketch*, on the other hand, suggests broad strokes—a clear outline without much precision of detail.

Scholars have been attempting this for over two hundred years in what Albert Schweitzer called "the quest for the historical Jesus." Throughout much of this century, as I indicated earlier, the scholarly effort to discern what the pre-Easter Jesus was like has been in eclipse, disparaged as historically impossible and theologically irrelevant; this period is referred to by historians of the discipline as the time of "no quest."

In the 1980s, however, in what has been called "a third quest for the historical Jesus," "a new era in Jesus research," and "a renaissance in Jesus scholarship," this has changed.[17] Now scholars are more confident that we can, with a reasonable degree of probability, know something about the historical

Jesus.[18] In the judgment of many, "a softly focused characterization" of the pre-Easter Jesus is possible.[19]

Two Negative Claims

Before I turn to my sketch, it is important that I make two negative statements. The first, which counters a central element in the popular image of Jesus, is that the self-understanding and message of the pre-Easter Jesus were in all likelihood *nonmessianic*. By this I mean simply that we have no way of knowing whether Jesus thought of himself as the Messiah or as the Son of God in some special sense. According to the earliest layers of the developing gospel tradition, he said nothing about having such thoughts. They were not part of his own teaching. His message was not about believing in him. Rather, the pre-Easter Jesus consistently pointed away from himself to God. His message was *theocentric*, not christocentric—centered in God, not centered in a messianic proclamation about himself.

The second negative statement, which counters a widespread scholarly image of Jesus, is that in all likelihood the pre-Easter Jesus was *noneschatological*. That statement needs precise formulation in order not to be misunderstood: what is being denied is the notion that Jesus expected the supernatural coming of the Kingdom of God as a world-ending event in his own generation.[20] This growing scholarly consensus is a recent development. Over the last ten years, the image of Jesus as an eschatological prophet, which dominated scholarship through the middle third of this century, has become very much a minority position.[21]

Four Positive Strokes

My own sketch of the pre-Easter Jesus consists of four broad strokes. It is based upon a typology of religious figures. My research and evaluation of the best Jesus scholarship convince me that Jesus had characteristics of several different types of religious personalities, and each stroke in my sketch identifies him with one of these types. Because I have developed this idea in considerable detail elsewhere, I will present it here very compactly.[22]

1. The historical Jesus was a *spirit person*, one of those figures in human history with an experiential awareness of the reality of God. I will say more about this later in this chapter.

2. Jesus was a *teacher of wisdom* who regularly used the classic forms of wisdom speech (parables, and memorable short sayings known as aphorisms) to teach a subversive and alternative wisdom. About this I will say more in chapter 4.

3. Jesus was a *social prophet*, similar to the classical prophets of ancient Israel. As such, he criticized the elites (economic, political, and religious) of his time, was an advocate of an alternative social vision, and was often in conflict with authorities. About this point I will say more in chapter 3.

4. Jesus was a *movement founder* who brought into being a Jewish renewal or revitalization movement that challenged and shattered the social boundaries of his day, a movement that eventually became the early Christian church. I will say more about this in chapter 3.

These four strokes, taken in combination with the two negative statements made earlier, provide a sketch or profile of what the pre-Easter Jesus was like.[23] Together, they enable us to constellate the traditions about him into a coherent whole. The outline is very skeletal, of course, and I wish to flesh it out. Without seeking to be comprehensive or developing them in detail, I want to describe some impressions of Jesus that have struck me over the years.

Some Impressions of Jesus

Jesus' verbal gifts were remarkable. His language was most often metaphorical, poetic, and imaginative, filled with memorable short sayings and compelling short stories. He was clearly exceptionally intelligent. Not only were his insights pointed and illuminating, but he was very clever in debate, often turning a question back on his interrogators so that they could not respond without discrediting themselves. In contemporary terms, he was gifted as both a right-brain and left-brain thinker.

He used dramatic public actions. He ate meals with untouchables, which not only generated criticism but also symbolized his alternative vision of human community. He entered Jerusalem at the head of a procession on a donkey—a virtual parody of prevailing ideas of kingship. Like the classical prophets of ancient Israel, he performed symbolic actions: on one occasion he provocatively staged a demonstration in the temple, overturning the tables of the money changers and driving out the sellers of sacrificial animals.

There was a radical social and political edge to his message and activity. He challenged the social order of his day and indicted the elites who dominated it. He had a clever tongue, which could playfully or sarcastically indict the powerful and proper. He must have been remarkably courageous, willing to continue what he was doing even when it was clear that it was putting him in lethal danger. The fate of his mentor John the Baptizer must have been a vivid reminder to him of what happened to unauthorized leaders who attracted a significant following in the tense political atmosphere of first-century Palestine.

He was a remarkable healer: more healing stories are told about him than about anybody else in the Jewish tradition. He attracted a following, including people who left their previous lives behind, and any sketch of Jesus with a claim to historical credibility must account for this fact.[24] There must have been something quite compelling about him. He also attracted enemies, especially among the rich and powerful.

And finally, he was young, his life was short, and his public activity was brief. He lived only into his early thirties, and his public activity lasted perhaps as little as a year (according to the synoptic gospels) or as much as three or four years (according to John). The founders of the world's other major religious traditions lived long lives and were active for decades. It is exceptional that so much came forth from such a brief life. He must have been a remarkable person. No wonder his followers are said to have exclaimed, "What manner of man is this?"

JESUS AS SPIRIT PERSON AND MEDIATOR OF THE SACRED

The first stroke in my four-stroke sketch is foundational to everything else Jesus was.[25] The most crucial fact about Jesus was that he was a "spirit person," a "mediator of the sacred," one of those persons in human history to whom the Spirit was an experiential reality.[26]

It took me a long time to see this. The process began with the realization that there really are such phenomena as experiences of Spirit and spirit persons. The realization came to me initially not from the study of the Bible or the Christian tradition, but from the study of non-Western religions and cultural anthropology. This illuminating category helps us see much about Jesus that we otherwise might miss.

We begin with what a spirit person is. The older, semitechnical term is *holy man*, but *spirit person* seems better. The change to *person* reflects the fact that such figures come in both genders, which makes a gender-inclusive term desirable. The change to *spirit* (*spirit* person rather than *holy* person) seeks to avoid the connotations of *holy*, which there is a natural tendency to understand as an adjective denoting a moral quality, such as *righteous* or *pious* or *revered* or *saintly* or even *sanctimonious*. Such a reading would profoundly obscure what the phrase is meant to convey: a person to whom the sacred is an experiential reality.[27]

Spirit persons are known cross-culturally. They are people who have vivid and frequent subjective experiences of another level or dimension of reality. These experiences involve momentary entry into nonordinary states of consciousness and take a number of different forms. Sometimes there is a vivid sense of momentarily seeing into another layer of reality; these are visionary experiences. Sometimes there is the experience of journeying into that other dimension of reality; this is the classic experience of the shaman. Sometimes there is a strong sense of another reality coming upon one, as in the ancient expression "The Spirit fell upon me." Sometimes the experience is of nature or an object within nature momentarily transfigured by "the sacred" shining through it. Bushes burn without being consumed; the whole earth is seen as filled with the glory of God (where *glory* means "radiant presence"). The world is perceived in such a way that previous perceptions seem nothing more than blindness.

What all persons who have these experiences share is a strong sense of there being more to reality than the tangible world of our ordinary experience. They share a compelling sense of having experienced something "real." They feel strongly that they know something they didn't know before. Their experiences are noetic, involving not simply a *feeling* of ecstasy, but a *knowing*. What such persons know is *the sacred*. Spirit persons are people who experience the sacred frequently and vividly.[28]

It is experiences such as these that have led the religious traditions of the world to speak of "the sacred." *The sacred* (or *the numinous*) refers to the other reality encountered in these experiences. Most often, of course, the religious traditions do not speak of the sacred abstractly; rather, they *name* it—as Yahweh, Brahman, Atman, Allah, the Tao, Great Spirit, God. This is not to suppose that all these names (and the concepts associated with them) mean the same thing.[29] But it is to suppose that the impulse to name something as sacred flows out of the experience of the sacred. Because the most common name for the sacred in the Jewish-Christian tradition is *God,* I shall from now on most often use *God* or *(the) Spirit* when referring to the sacred.

Spirit persons share a second feature as well: they become mediators of the sacred. They mediate the Spirit in various ways. Sometimes they speak the word or will of God. Sometimes they mediate the power of God in the form of healings and/or exorcisms. Sometimes they function as game finders or rainmakers in hunting-and-gathering and early agricultural societies. Sometimes they become charismatic warriors or military leaders. What they all have in common is that they become funnels or conduits for the power or wisdom of God to enter into this world. Anthropologically speaking, they are delegates of the tribe to another layer of reality, mediators who connect their communities to the Spirit.

It is important to note that the experience of spirit persons presupposes an understanding of reality very different from the dominant image of reality in the modern Western world. The modern worldview, derived from the Enlightenment, sees reality in material terms, as constituted by the world of matter and energy within the space-time continuum. The experience of spirit persons suggests that there is more to reality than this— that there is, in addition to the tangible world of our ordinary experience, a nonmaterial level of reality, actual even though nonmaterial, and charged with energy and power. The modern worldview is one-dimensional; the worldview of spirit persons is multidimensional.

Moreover, this other reality, it is important to emphasize, is not "somewhere else." Rather, it is all around us, and we are in it. In William James's words, we are separated from it only by filmy screens of consciousness.[30] When those screens of consciousness momentarily drop away, the experience of Spirit occurs. A spirit person is one in whom those screens of consciousness are unusually permeable—compared with most of us, who seem to have hardened rinds of consciousness instead.

Judaism had its stream of spirit persons. Indeed, they are the central figures in the biblical tradition, going back to the beginnings of Israel. Abraham and Jacob had visions of God and other paranormal experiences. Moses was a spirit person par excellence. He ascended Mount Sinai—the sacred mountain that symbolically is the navel of the earth, the *axis mundi* connecting this world to the other world—and there was in intimate communion with God. According to the book of Exodus, when he came down from the mountain his face even glowed with the divine presence. I have no idea if things such as that happen or not, but the point of the tradition is clear: Moses is presented as one of these mediators. He "knew God face to face," as his brief obituary at the end of the book of Deuteronomy puts it.[31]

Beyond Moses there is Elijah, a social prophet who was experientially in touch with the Spirit of God. He even, according to the stories about him, "journeyed in the Spirit," much as the Sioux spirit person Black Elk is reported to have done. Then there are the prophets of ancient Israel. For most of them the story of their "call" is told, typically involving a visionary experience of another reality. Classic among these is the story of Ezekiel, whose book begins with words that almost make the hairs on the back of one's neck stand up: "In the thirtieth year, in the fourth month of the year, on the fifth day of the month, by the river Chebar, *the heavens were opened and I saw visions of God.*"

Closer to the time of Jesus there were a number of Jewish holy men or spirit persons. Best known are Honi the Circle-

Drawer and Hanina ben Dosa, both of whom were famed for their contemplative prayer and their ability as "miracle workers."[32] If we move beyond Jesus for just a moment, the Pharisee Saul became the apostle Paul through his experience of the Spirit. According to the book of Acts, he had a vision on the Damascus Road that involved both a *photism* (an experience of light) and an *audition* (a voice).[33] According to Paul himself, he had a vivid experience of journeying into "the third heaven" and there experiencing things that are unutterable, that may not be put into words because they transcend the categories of language.[34]

It seems to me that, given that there really are spirit persons and that the Jewish tradition included many such figures, Jesus was clearly a spirit person. The stories of his life in the gospels make this very clear. He had visions, including a vision at his baptism in which, like Ezekiel, he "saw the heavens opened" and the Spirit descending upon him like a dove.[35] That vision was followed by a series of visions in the wilderness in what we typically call the temptation narrative, but which a cultural anthropologist would recognize immediately as a wilderness ordeal or vision quest, characteristic of spirit persons.[36]

Jesus used spiritual practices, including both fasting and prayer. We are told that he prayed for hours at a time, sometimes all night long, and presumably not because his prayer list had gotten exceptionally long. Rather, it seems more likely that he practiced a form of contemplation or meditation similar to that of Hanina ben Dosa and Honi the Circle-Drawer. About them it is said in the Jewish tradition that they would still their hearts before God before they would heal. The practice of wordless meditation is not simply an Eastern tradition, but is central to the Jewish-Christian tradition as well.

Other indicators that Jesus was a spirit person include the intimate way in which he addressed God. In particular, he called God *Abba*, which is the Aramaic word that a toddler on the babbling edge of speech uses to address his or her father. It is like the English *papa*. So Jesus called God "Papa" (he also, as we shall see in subsequent chapters, referred to God with female imagery). Why would a first-century Jewish person address God as "Papa" when his tradition typically used much more formal terms of address for God? It is a bit shocking, and Jesus may have used this word for that reason, of course. That would be quite in character. But it also seems likely that this intimate term of address for God expressed the intimacy of Jesus' own experience of God.

Jesus spoke with "authority," which is best understood as flowing out of his own spiritual experience. It was not the authority of "Thus says the Lord," but rather an authority that took the form of "You have heard it said of old, but I say unto you. . . ." Sometimes his sayings began with the word *amen* rather than ending with it. This initial *amen* is unusual within Judaism. Such authoritative forms of speaking suggest that he perceived himself as speaking "from the mouth of the Spirit," and not simply as reciting tradition.[37]

According to some of the stories in the gospels, his followers experienced a presence around him that was palpable and contagious. This seems similar to the spiritual presence or zone of liberation that other famous religious figures such as the Buddha and Saint Francis of Assisi are reported to have generated. Of course, Jesus was both a healer and an exorcist. Modern scholars generally accept that there is a historical core to the healing and exorcism stories, even though we may not be confident that any particular story is a detailed report of a specific incident. But historically speaking, we can say that Jesus was perceived by his contemporaries and himself as an exorcist who cast demons out of people and as a healer of diseases, and that this was attributed to the power of the Spirit working through him.

All of this makes it plausible to locate Jesus' own spirituality within what we know of Jewish mysticism in his day. Our picture of early Jewish mysticism has been growing, especially in the last several years.[38] The more we realize that there was a form of Jewish mysticism in first-century Palestine, the more likely it seems that Jesus stood in that experiential tradition.[39]

Jesus' experience of the Spirit is expressed with dramatic simplicity in the "inaugural address" in Luke with which he begins his ministry: *"The Spirit of the Lord is upon me."*[40] At the center of Jesus' life was a profound and continuous relationship to the Spirit of God.

IMPLICATIONS FOR THE LIFE OF THE CHURCH

This understanding of Jesus as a spirit person has significant implications for the life of the church today. It affects how we see Jesus, God, and the Christian life.

The image of the pre-Easter Jesus as one who experienced God is quite different from common understandings of Jesus. It is very different from my childhood image of Jesus as one who was God, an understanding that is still held by some in the church and that surfaces in the question "Do you believe Jesus was God?" The image of Jesus sketched in this chapter suggests that the answer is "No, the pre-Easter Jesus was not God."[41] It is also quite different from the image of Jesus as one who believed strongly (and perhaps wrongly) in God, which was how I thought of Jesus in my early adulthood. The sketch of Jesus as a spirit person suggests that Jesus was not simply a person who believed strongly in God, but one who knew God.

The sketch affects how we see Jesus in another way as well. Imaging Jesus as a particular instance of a type of religious personality known cross-culturally undermines a widespread Christian belief that Jesus is unique, which most commonly is linked to the notion that Christianity is exclusively true and that Jesus is "the only way."[42] The image I have sketched views Jesus differently: rather than being the exclusive revelation of God, he is one of many mediators of the sacred. Yet even as this view subtracts from the uniqueness of Jesus and the Christian tradition, it also in my judgment adds to the credibility of both.

To speak personally, when the truth of the Christian tradition was tied to the claim that the revelation of God was found only in this tradition (and in the antecedent Jewish tradition), there came a time when its truth became for me highly unlikely. What are the chances that God would speak only to and through this particular group of people (who just happened to be *our* group of people)? Indeed, I can put it more strongly: it became impossible for me to believe this. However, I find the image of Jesus as a spirit person highly credible. There really are people like this—and Jesus was one of them. There really are experiences of the sacred, of the numinous, of God—and Jesus was one for whom God was an experiential reality.

This leads to a second set of implications, which concern how we think of God. Candor compels me to acknowledge that experiences of the sacred do not prove the reality of God (though I find them far more interesting and convincing than any of the "proofs" for the existence of God). But if one does take these experiences as epiphanies of the way things are, as disclosures of the sacred—as I do myself—they have implications for how we think of God.

They challenge our most common ways of thinking about God and invite us into a much different way of imaging God. The most common modern understandings of God in the church (as well as in our culture) are deist or supernaturalist. Speaking broadly, the deist way conceives of God as a supernatural being "out there" who created the world a long time ago, who established natural laws as a way of ordering it, and who no longer has much to do with it. The supernaturalist way of imaging God also sees God as a being "out there," and differs from deism only by affirming that God from time to time supernaturally intervenes in this world (especially in the events reported in the Old and New Testaments). Different as the two views are, they have some things in common. Both are products of the Enlightenment, which removed God from this world.[43] Both are instances of "the god of theism," which images God as a being separate from the world—that is, as a primarily transcendent reality. And both typically stress belief as the basis for affirming the existence of a God who is essentially not around.

The image of God that goes with the understanding of Jesus as a spirit person is very different. Rather than being an article of belief, God becomes an experiential reality. The Jewish tradition in which Jesus stood speaks of persons who "know" God, and the Hebrew word for *know* is the same word used for sexual intercourse. God can be *known* in that direct and intimate way, not merely believed in. The experience of spirit persons in general and of Jesus in particular suggests that God is not to be thought of as a remote and transcendent creator far removed from this world, but imaged as all around us—as "the one in whom we live and move and have our being," as the book of Acts puts it in words attributed to Saint Paul.[44] Within this framework, the pre-Easter Jesus becomes a powerful testimony to the reality and knowability of God.

Finally, the image of Jesus as a spirit person has implications for how we think of the Christian life. It shifts the focus of the Christian life from believing in Jesus or believing in God to being in relationship to the same Spirit that Jesus knew. It is the claim that I emphasized at the end of chapter 1 and that will emerge yet again in this book: that the Christian life moves beyond believing in God to being in relationship to God.

NOTES

1. The first stage of the Jesus Seminar's work (on the *sayings* of Jesus) is about to be published in a color-coded edition of the gospels, in which sayings of Jesus will be printed in the four colors that correspond to the Seminar's voting: *The Five Gospels: The Search for the Authentic Words of Jesus* (New York: Macmillan, scheduled for publication in early 1994; the fifth gospel is Thomas). The second stage of the Seminar's work, now under way, focuses on the *deeds* of Jesus.

2. See Helmut Koester and Stephen J. Patterson, "The Gospel of Thomas: Does It Contain Authentic Sayings of Jesus?" *Bible Review,* April 1990, pp. 26–39. See also Stevan Davies, *The Gospel of Thomas and Christian Wisdom* (New York: Seabury, 1983); John S. Kloppenborg et al., *Q Thomas Reader* (Sonoma, CA: Polebridge, 1990); and Marvin Meyer, *The Gospel of Thomas* (San Francisco, HarperSanFrancisco: 1992).

3. See, for example, Elisabeth Schüssler Fiorenza, *In Memory of Her* (New York: Crossroad, 1985), pp. 105–6, where the author tells about a friend who had to work very hard to convince an adult education class in her parish that Jesus was Jewish, only to have somebody respond, "But the Blessed Mother for sure is not."

4. Translation from E. Hennecke and W. Schneemelcher, *New Testament Apocrypha* (Philadelphia: Westminster, 1963, 1965), vol. 1, p. 393. In the episode immediately preceding this one, Jesus says to another child, "You insolent godless dunderhead, . . . you shall wither like a tree and shall bear neither leaves nor root nor fruit," and the child "immediately withered up completely." The Infancy Gospel of Thomas (as well as all other early Christian gospels) is now most easily accessible in *The Complete Gospels*, ed. Robert J. Miller (Sonoma, CA: Polebridge, 1992).

5. Luke's account of Jesus amazing the teachers in the temple at age twelve probably represents an early stage of this process.

6. Legends have sought to fill in the missing or "silent" years of Jesus. Suggestions abound that he traveled to India, or encountered Buddhist missionaries in Alexandria in Egypt, or studied magic with Egyptian magicians, or was part of the Qumran community on the shores of the Dead Sea. But all such suggestions are extremely hypothetical speculations, about which one might say, "It is possible (virtually anything is possible), but why should one think so?" We can account for everything we see in Jesus without needing to hypothesize influences from outside of the Jewish tradition.

7. And he was probably born in Nazareth, not Bethlehem. Such is the natural inference from the name by which he is known: Jesus of Nazareth. The tradition that he was born in Bethlehem is probably part of the symbol making of the early Christian movement, which associated Jesus as "Messiah" and "Son of David" with the promise of a Davidic ruler who would come from the "city of David"—that is, Bethlehem. See Micah 5.2–4 and its use in Matthew 2.5–6. For a careful current treatment of this question and of the conclusion that Jesus was probably born in Nazareth, see John P. Meier, *A Marginal Jew: Rethinking the Historical Jesus* (New York: Doubleday, 1991), vol. 1, pp. 214–16.

8. The basis for this judgment is that Joseph is not mentioned during the ministry, though Jesus' mother and siblings are. The tradition that Joseph was an old man when he married Mary has no foundation in the New Testament itself; it perhaps was created to make more plausible the later tradition about the perpetual virginity of Mary.

9. Some contemporary scholars are skeptical about whether there were synagogues in Galilee at the time of Jesus, primarily because of the ambiguity of archaeological evidence for the existence of synagogue buildings from that time. The word *synagogue*, however, means simply "assembly" and need not refer to a building constructed especially for that purpose. Thus the question of whether there were synagogue *buildings* should not be confused with the question of whether there were synagogue assemblies. That there were assemblies in which teaching and worship occurred seems clear.

10. It is interesting to note that this widely accepted "fact" about Jesus is based on only a slim half verse in the gospels.

11. This term is used by E. P. Sanders in *Judaism: Practice and Belief, 63 B.C.E.–66 C.E.* (Philadelphia: Trinity Press International, 1992). For

another important recent study of the first-century Jewish world, see N. Thomas Wright, *The New Testament and the People of God* (Minneapolis: Fortress, 1992), pp. 145–338. For illumination of the social world of Jesus as reflected in the gospels, see the very helpful new book by Bruce J. Malina and Richard L. Rohrbaugh, *Social-Science Commentary on the Synoptic Gospels* (Minneapolis: Fortress, 1992). See also Frederick J. Murphy, *The Religious World of Jesus: An Introduction to Second Temple Palestinian Judaism* (Nashville, TN: Abingdon, 1991).

12. For a more comprehensive discussion of the Jewish festivals, see Sanders, *Judaism*, pp. 125–43.

13. The Shema consists of Deuteronomy 6.4–5: "Hear O Israel: The LORD is our God, the LORD alone. You shall love the LORD your God with all your heart, and with all your soul, and with all your might." The twice-daily prayers apparently included the recitation of a number of biblical passages in addition to Deuteronomy 6.4–5. For a discussion of prayer practice, see Sanders, *Judaism*, pp. 195–208.

14. William James, *The Varieties of Religious Experience,* ed. Martin Marty (New York: Penguin, 1982; originally published in 1902), pp. 189–258.

15. Matthew 11.11 = Luke 7.28.

16. For example, John Dominic Crossan has speculated that John's execution led Jesus to rethink central aspects of the message that he learned from John. Many scholars have noted that Jesus' message differs in major ways from what we know of John's message (including, according to Crossan, a shift from an apocalyptic to a non-apocalyptic understanding of the Kingdom of God), and it is possible that the differences are (at least in part) the result of the trauma caused by John's execution by the rulers of this world.

17. The phrases are from, respectively, N. Thomas Wright in Wright and Stephen Neill, *The Interpretation of the New Testament* (New York: Oxford Univ. Press, 1988), pp. 379–403; James H. Charlesworth, *Jesus Within Judaism* (New York: Doubleday, 1988), pp. 9–29; and Marcus J. Borg, "A Renaissance in Jesus Studies," *Theology Today* 45 (1988), pp. 280–92.

18. E. P. Sanders, *Jesus and Judaism* (Philadelphia: Fortress, 1985), p. 2.

19. The phrase comes from Burton L. Mack, *A Myth of Innocence: Mark and Christian Origins* (Philadelphia: Fortress, 1988), p. 56. Mack might fairly be viewed as the most skeptical of major contemporary Jesus scholars, and thus it is significant that he affirms this possibility.

20. Thus scholars who understand the word *eschatological* differently might continue to affirm an eschatological understanding of Jesus. See the essays cited in n. 21.

21. For a more complete report of this development, see my essays "A Temperate Case for a Non-Eschatological Jesus," published simultaneously in *Foundations and Facets Forum* 2, no. 3 (1986), pp. 81–102, and in *Society of Biblical Literature: 1986 Seminar Papers* (Atlanta: Scholars Press, 1986), pp. 521–35; "A Renaissance in Jesus Studies," *Theology Today* 45 (1988), pp. 280–92; "Portraits of Jesus in Contemporary North American Scholarship," *Harvard Theological Review* 84 (1991), pp. 1–22; and "Jesus and Eschatology: A Re-Assessment," an essay in a volume edited by James Charlesworth to be published by Trinity Press International late in 1993.

22. See my book *Jesus: A New Vision* (San Francisco: Harper & Row, 1987).

23. To relate this sketch of the adult Jesus to the voting of the Jesus Seminar: the two negative claims and the "stroke" portraying Jesus as a teacher of a subversive wisdom are supported by strong majorities within the Seminar; indeed, they are near-consensus positions. On the other three "strokes," the Seminar is about equally divided, pointing to lack of consensus and suggesting that these are likely to be central questions within the discipline over the next several years.

24. Its inability to account for this fact is, it seems to me, the major problem with the film of a few years ago *The Last Temptation of Christ*. For me, its most problematic aspect was not sexuality, but its portrayal of Jesus as a somewhat bumbling figure who was not even very good at telling parables. Why would anyone follow such a Jesus?

25. For a fuller treatment of much of the material in this section, see Borg, *Jesus: A New Vision*, pp. 25–75.

26. I use the phrase *the Spirit* in as generic a sense as possible, and not in the specifically Christian sense of the (Holy) Spirit. By *the Spirit* I mean *the sacred*, understood as that nonmaterial reality or presence that is experienced in extraordinary moments. Religious traditions name it in various ways. In Christian terms, *Spirit* is synonymous with *God*, so long as God is understood as an experiential reality and not as a distant being.

27. Though *spirit person* sometimes strikes me as an odd phrase, it seems superior to its possible alternatives. I have already suggested why *holy person* is not satisfactory. *Sacred person* is another possibility; it

would work if clearly understood to mean "a person in touch with the Sacred." Yet I think *sacred person* would most commonly be understood to mean "divine person," and therefore easily be misunderstood as referring to the divinity of Jesus.

28. This other layer of reality is experienced as transpersonal. That is, though it is known in one's own subjectivity, it is experienced as transcending the boundaries of one's own person. This transpersonal realm is what I mean by a world of Spirit. The ways of imaging or conceptualizing it range from Martin Buber's "I-Thou," in which the divine "Thou" is mediated perhaps wholly through the world of the everyday, to Mircea Eliade's distinction between the sacred and the profane, to the world of the Jungian archetypes, to the shamanistic cosmology of another world filled with a multiplicity of spirits.

29. I agree with those who speak of each religious tradition as a "cultural-linguistic world"; see, for example, George Lindbeck, *The Nature of Doctrine* (Philadelphia: Westminster, 1984). Thus the religions of the world are clearly not all the same; they are as different as the cultures out of which they come. Yet I remain convinced that the impetus for creating these cultural-linguistic worlds comes out of certain kinds of extraordinary experiences that are cross-cultural.

30. James, *Varieties of Religious Experience*, p. 388.

31. Deuteronomy 34.10.

32. Geza Vermes, *Jesus the Jew* (New York: Macmillan, 1973), pp. 58–82. This remains the classic work on Jewish holy men. Though some of Vermes's conclusions have been qualified by subsequent research (see especially William Scott Green, "Palestinian Holy Men: Charismatic Leadership and Rabbinic Tradition," *Aufstieg und Niedergang der Römischen Welt* 2.19.619–47), his central claim that there were Jewish figures such as these roughly contemporary with Jesus continues to seem solid.

33. For a discussion of "photisms" as sometimes accompanying sudden conversion experiences, see James, *Varieties of Religious Experience*, pp. 251–53.

34. 2 Corinthians 12.1–4. See James D. Tabor, *Things Unutterable* (Lanham, MD: Univ. Press of America, 1986); and Alan E. Segal, *Paul the Convert: The Apostolate and Apostasy of Saul the Pharisee* (New Haven, CT: Yale Univ. Press, 1990), especially pp. 34–71.

35. Mark 1.10, RSV.

36. I am aware of the difficulties involved in reading the stories of Jesus' baptismal and wilderness visions as historical accounts. Many scholars would assign them to the developing tradition in the post-Easter period. Yet it is worth noting that they are to be found, respectively, in Mark and Q, both of which are early layers of the gospel tradition. Minimally, this means that the tradition at an early stage of development presents Jesus as one who had visions. We may view this either as invention or as faithful representation of something that was true about Jesus. If invention, one must ask, "To what end?" Was there a felt need to legitimate or "elevate" Jesus by reporting experiences of the Spirit? Though certainty is impossible, it seems more plausible to say that Jesus (like so many figures before and after him in the Jewish-Christian tradition) had visions. Interestingly, the Jesus Seminar, typically quite skeptical about such texts, was divided about evenly on the question of whether Jesus had visions (in a vote that took place at the group's spring 1992 meeting).

37. For more on "speaking from the mouth of the Spirit" in the Jewish tradition, see Borg, *Jesus: A New Vision*, p. 46 and n. 34.

38. For a compact treatment of early Jewish mysticism, see Segal, *Paul the Convert*.

39. See John Dominic Crossan's brief remark in "Materials and Methods in Historical Jesus Research," *Forum* 4, no. 4 (December 1988), p. 11: Jesus' message of "the unmediated presence of God . . . was based on mystical experience, since I have no idea where else it might have come from."

40. Here also I am aware of the historical difficulties involved in saying that Luke actually reports what Jesus said at the outset of his ministry. Yet I would make the claim that, whether the scene reported in Luke 4.16–19 is historical or a literary construction created by Luke, it accurately reflects the fact that Jesus experienced himself as one anointed by the Spirit.

41. This denial does not preclude affirming that Jesus was an epiphany or disclosure of God, or, as I will suggest in chapter 5, the embodiment or incarnation of the Word and Wisdom of God. See also *Jesus: A New Vision*, pp. 191–92.

42. To amplify slightly, I would agree that Jesus is unique in one sense of the word, and deny that he is unique in another. In the sense that Jesus is not exactly like any other religious figure, he is unique (and so are the Buddha, Muhammad, Lao-tzu, and, for that matter, every

person). But in popular Christian usage, the "uniqueness" of Jesus is most commonly tied to the notion that he is the uniquely and exclusively true revelation of God. It is this meaning of his uniqueness that I deny.

43. The Enlightenment is the "great divide" in Western intellectual history that separates the modern period from all that went before it. The Enlightenment began in the seventeenth century and gave birth to the modern worldview with its understanding of reality as material and "self-contained," operating in accord with "natural laws" of cause and effect. For its effects on religion, see W. T. Stace, *Religion and the Modern Mind* (Philadelphia: Lippincott, 1952); and Huston Smith, *Forgotten Truth: The Primordial Tradition* (San Francisco: Harper & Row, 1976; 2d ed., 1992), especially chap. 1.

44. Acts 17.28.

3

Jesus, Compassion, and Politics

Two key words enable us to glimpse what was most central to Jesus: *Spirit* and *compassion*. As two focal points around which an image of Jesus may be constellated, they disclose what was most important to him. In the previous chapter, we treated the role of the Spirit in his life. In this chapter, we shall look at the centrality of compassion for him, as well as the significant ways in which Spirit and compassion are related to each other. Jesus' advocacy of compassion continues to be an invitation and a challenge to the church in our day.

Compassion is a particularly important word in the gospels. The stories told about Jesus speak of him as having compassion and of his being moved with compassion. The word also represents the summation of his teaching about both God and ethics. For Jesus, compassion was the central quality of God and the central moral quality of a life centered in God. These two aspects of compassion are combined most clearly and compactly in a single verse, to which we will return several times in this chapter:

Be compassionate as God is compassionate.[1]

This crystallization of Jesus' message speaks of a way of life grounded in an *imitatio dei*—an imitation of God. Image of God and ethos—what God is like and how we are to live—are brought together. Moreover, for Jesus compassion was not simply an individual virtue, but a sociopolitical paradigm expressing his alternative vision of human life in community, a vision of life embodied in the movement that came into existence around him.

THE MEANING OF COMPASSION

In the Hebrew Bible, which Christians typically call the Old Testament and which was sacred Scripture for Jesus and his Jewish contemporaries, the word *compassion* has rich semantic associations. In Hebrew (as well as in Aramaic), the word usually translated as "compassion" is the plural of a noun that in its singular form means "womb."[2] In the Hebrew Bible, *compassion* is both a feeling and a way of being that flows out of that feeling. Sometimes it is very specifically linked to its association with *womb:* a woman feels compassion for the child of her own womb; a man feels compassion for his brother, who comes from the same womb.[3] As a feeling, compassion is located in a certain part of the body—namely, in the loins. In women, as one would expect, this means in the womb;[4] in men, in the bowels.[5] Thus we have that somewhat odd biblical expression "his bowels were moved with compassion." But obviously it is the same part of the body.

In terms of feeling, *compassion* means "to feel with," as even the etymology of the English word suggests: *-passion* comes from the Latin word that means "to feel," and the prefix *com-* means "with." Compassion thus means feeling the feelings of somebody else in a visceral way, at a level somewhere below the level of the head; most commonly compassion is associated with feeling the suffering of somebody else and being moved by that suffering to do something. That is, the feeling of compassion leads to being compassionate.

Quite often the Hebrew words for *compassion* and *compassionate* are translated into English as *mercy* and *merciful*. But compassion is quite different from mercy, and being compassionate quite different from being merciful. In English *mercy* and *merciful* most commonly imply a superior in relationship to a subordinate, and also a situation of wrongdoing: one is merciful toward somebody to whom one has the right (or power) to act otherwise. *Compassion* suggests something else. To paraphrase William Blake, mercy wears a human face, and compassion a human heart.

COMPASSION, GOD, AND ETHICS

The Hebrew word for "compassion" whose singular form means "womb" is often used of God in the Old Testament. It is translated as "merciful" in the characterization of God as "gracious and merciful."[6] It is present in that quite wonderful expression from the King James Bible the "tender mercies" of God.[7] It is found in a passage in Jeremiah that has been translated as follows:

> Thus says Yahweh:
> Is Ephraim [Israel] my dear son? my darling child?
> For the more I speak of him,
> the more I do remember him.
> Therefore my womb trembles for him;
> I will truly show motherly-compassion upon him.[8]

Thus the Hebrew Bible speaks frequently of God as compassionate, with resonances of "womb" close at hand.

And so Jesus' statement "Be compassionate *as God is compassionate*" is rooted in the Jewish tradition. As an image for the central quality of God, it is striking. To say that God is compassionate is to say that God is "like a womb," is "womblike," or, to coin a word that captures the flavor of the original Hebrew, "wombish." What does it suggest to say that God is like a womb? Metaphoric and evocative, the phrase and its associated image provocatively suggest a number of connotations. Like a womb, God is the one who gives birth to us—the mother who gives birth to us. As a mother loves the children of her womb and feels for the children of her womb, so God loves us and feels for us, for all of her children. In its sense of "like a womb," *compassionate* has nuances of giving life, nourishing, caring, perhaps embracing and encompassing. For Jesus, this is what God is like.[9]

And, to complete the *imitatio dei*, to "be compassionate as God is compassionate" is to be like a womb as God is like a womb. It is to feel as God feels and to act as God acts: in a life-giving and nourishing way. "To be compassionate" is what is meant elsewhere in the New Testament by the somewhat more abstract command "to love." According to Jesus, compassion is to be the central quality of a life faithful to God the compassion-ate one.

COMPASSION, SOCIAL WORLD, AND POLITICS

Though compassion as the content of Jesus' *imitatio dei* was rooted in the Jewish tradition, it was not the dominant *imitatio dei* of the first-century Jewish social world. Instead, a different *imitatio dei*, also grounded in the Hebrew Bible, had become the primary paradigm shaping the Jewish social world: "Be holy as God is holy."[10]

It is in the conflict between these two *imitatio deis*—between holiness and compassion as qualities of God to be embodied in community—that we see the central conflict in the ministry of Jesus: between two different social visions. The dominant social vision was centered in holiness; the alternative social vision of Jesus was centered in compassion.

Indeed, it is only when we appreciate this dimension of Jesus' emphasis upon compassion that we realize how radical his message and vision were. For Jesus, compassion was more than a quality of God and an individual virtue: it was a social paradigm, the core value for life in community. To put it boldly: compassion for Jesus was political. He directly and repeatedly challenged the dominant sociopolitical paradigm of his social world and advocated instead what might be called a *politics of compassion*.[11] This conflict and this social vision continue to have striking implications for the life of the church today.

To see this, we need to look at the role that purity played in Jesus' social world. He was often in conflict with his critics about purity laws and issues. Within the modern church, we tend to view such disputes as trivial, seeing purity laws as part of the ritual or ceremonial law of ancient Judaism, and of little importance compared with the moral law. We wonder how any reasonably thoughtful person could be concerned about such matters, which strike us as rather silly. Moreover, we tend to think of purity in individualistic terms, as if it were something that an overly pious individual might become meticulous about. But in first-century Jewish Palestine, this was not the case. Purity was neither trivial nor individualistic. Rather, to put it concisely, purity was political.

The Purity System of the Jewish Social World

Purity was political because it structured society into a purity system. It took as its starting point the verse briefly mentioned earlier:

> Speak to all the congregation of the people of Israel and say to them: *You shall be holy, for I the LORD your God am holy.*[12]

As an *imitatio dei*, the passage joins together an image of God and an ethos for the community: God is holy; therefore Israel is to be holy. Moreover, holiness was understood to mean "separation from everything unclean." Holiness thus meant the same as purity, and the passage was thus understood as, "You [Israel] shall be pure as God is pure." The ethos of purity produced a politics of purity—that is, a society structured around a purity system.

Purity systems are found in many cultures. At a high level of abstraction, they are systems of classifications, lines and boundaries. A purity system "is a cultural map which indicates 'a place for everything and everything in its place.'"[13] Things that are okay in one place are impure or dirty in another, where they are out of place. Slightly more narrowly, and put very simply, a purity system is a social system organized around the contrasts or polarities of pure and impure, clean and unclean.[14] The polarities of pure and impure establish a spectrum or "purity map" ranging from pure on one end through varying degrees of purity to impure (or "off the purity map") at the other. These polarities apply to persons, places, things, times, and social groups.

Most important for our purposes is the way "pure" and "impure" applied to persons and social groups in the first-century Jewish social world. The purity system established a spectrum of people ranging from the pure through varying degrees of purity to people on the margin to the radically impure.

One's purity status depended to some extent on birth. According to one purity map of the time, priests and Levites (both hereditary classes) come first, followed by "Israelites," followed by "converts" (Jewish persons who were not Jewish by birth). Further down the list are "bastards," followed by those with damaged testicles and those without a penis.[15]

But one's degree of purity or impurity also depended on behavior.[16] Those who were carefully observant of the purity codes were "the pure," of course. The worst of the nonobservant were "outcasts." They included occupational groups such as tax collectors and perhaps shepherds (which provides a fresh perspective on the shepherds in Luke's account of Jesus' birth: the news of the birth comes to outcasts).[17] "The righteous" were those who followed the purity system, and "sinners" were those who did not. Though the word *sinners* had a range of meanings in first-century Palestine, it was not understood to include everybody (as it does in the mainstream Christian theological tradition),[18] but rather referred to particular groups of people, the worst of whom were "untouchables."[19] Parenthetically, it is interesting to note what happens to the notion of sin within a purity system. Sin becomes a matter of being impure or "dirty" and renders one "untouchable." This connection between sin and impurity is preserved in some Christian confessions of sin that speak of being "sinful and unclean." So it was in first-century Judaism: *sinners* often meant "the impure."

The polarities of the purity system got attached to other contrasts as well. Physical wholeness was associated with purity, and lack of wholeness with impurity. People who were not "whole"—the maimed, the chronically ill, lepers, eunuchs, and so forth—were on the impure side of the spectrum. The purity contrast also was associated with economic class. To be sure, being rich did not automatically put one on the pure side (and first-century Judaism could speak of rich people who were wicked), but being abjectly poor almost certainly made one impure. To some extent, this association resulted from popular wisdom, which saw wealth as a blessing from God ("The righteous will prosper") and poverty as an indication that one had not lived right. And to some extent, it arose because the abject poor could not in practice observe the purity laws.[20]

Purity and impurity also were associated with the contrast between male and female. As with the wealthy, there was nothing about being a male that made one automatically pure; clearly, there were men who were outcasts. And there was nothing about being a woman that automatically made one impure. But generally speaking, men in their natural state were thought to be more pure than women. The natural bodily processes of childbirth and menstruation were considered sources of impurity, and these led to a more generalized sense of the impurity of women.[21] This is consistent with the status of women in that culture as distinctly second-class people, a point to which we shall return later in this chapter.

Finally, the polarity of pure and impure also was attached to whether one was a Jew or a Gentile. Being Jewish did not guarantee one's purity, of course. But by definition, all Gentiles were impure and unclean. Indeed, the ideology of purity contributed to the fact that Jesus lived in a generation headed toward war. Palestine was occupied territory, a colony of the Roman Empire, controlled by an impure and unclean Gentile oppressor; the purity system was one of the causes of the heroic but catastrophic Jewish revolt of A.D. 66, which ended in the destruction of Jerusalem in A.D. 70.

To sum up, the effect of the purity system was to create a world with sharp social boundaries: between pure and impure, righteous and sinner, whole and not whole, male and female, rich and poor, Jew and Gentile. There is one more point to be made before turning to Jesus' response to the purity system: the extent to which the system was dominant in the Jewish social world.

At the center of the purity system were the temple and the priesthood. The temple was the geographic and cultic center of Israel's purity map.[22] Its priests were therefore bound by the more stringent purity rules, which applied to those nearest the center of purity. Moreover, the income of both temple and priests (and Levites) depended upon the observance of purity laws by others. That income flowed largely from "tithes"—in effect, taxes on agricultural produce. Tithing was closely linked to purity; untithed produce was thus impure and would not be purchased by the observant.[23] So temple and priesthood had economic as well as religious interests in the purity system.

It should be added that the temple was also the center of the ruling elites among the Jewish people. Not only were the high priestly families the religious elite, but they overlapped the economic and political elites, being linked with them by frequent intermarriage and other associations. Thus the politics of purity was to some extent the ideology of the dominant elites—religious, political, and economic.

Purity was also central to two Jewish renewal groups in first-century Palestine. The Pharisees sought the extension of the more stringent priestly rules of purity into everyday life;[24] and the Essenes (probably still to be identified with the people of Qumran and the Dead Sea Scrolls, though this is not completely certain) withdrew to the desert wilderness along the Dead Sea, believing that purity could be attained only in isolation from the impure world of culture.[25]

We do not know the extent to which ordinary Jews were concerned about observing purity laws.[26] No doubt some did, while others ignored them; still others may have felt victimized by them (and therefore resentful toward the purity system and those who benefited from it). But we can say that both "temple Judaism" and the leading renewal movements were committed to the paradigm of purity. It was both a hermeneutic and social system: it formed the lens through which they saw sacred tradition and provided a map for ordering their world.

Jesus' Attack upon the Purity System

It is in the context of a purity system that created a world with sharp social boundaries between pure and impure, righteous and sinner, whole and not whole, male and female, rich and poor, Jew and Gentile, that we can see the sociopolitical significance of compassion. In the message and activity of Jesus, we see an alternative social vision: a community shaped not by the ethos and politics of purity, but by the ethos and politics of compassion.

The challenge is signaled at the outset by the *imitatio dei* of which Jesus speaks. It is striking that "Be compassionate as God is compassionate" so closely echoes "Be holy as God is holy," even as it makes a radical substitution. The close parallel suggests that Jesus deliberately replaced the core value of purity with compassion. Compassion, not holiness, is the dominant quality of God, and is therefore to be the ethos of the community that mirrors God.

Many of Jesus' sayings indicted the purity system. He criticized a system that emphasized tithing and neglected justice: "But woe to you Pharisees! For you tithe mint and rue and every herb, and neglect justice and the love of God."[27] Tithes on produce amounted to taxes paid to the priests and temple, and untithed produce was impure. Thus, in the name of purity, the meticulous payment of tithes was insisted upon, to the neglect of justice.

He called the Pharisees "unmarked graves which people walk over without knowing it," a criticism that might seem obscure to us.[28] The key is that corpses (and therefore burial places) were a source of severe impurity. To call the Pharisees "unmarked graves" is stunningly ironic: they were a movement seeking the extension of purity laws, and Jesus declared them to be instead a source of impurity.

Jesus spoke of purity as on the inside and not on the outside: "There is nothing outside a person that by going in can defile, but the things that come out are what defile."[29] To say that purity is a matter of what is inside is radically to subvert a purity system constituted by external boundaries.

The same point is made by another saying: "Blessed are the pure in heart."[30] When I was growing up, I heard this saying as an impossible demand, thinking, "Oh my God, I'm supposed to be pure in heart! If I just had to be pure on the outside, I could maybe handle it, but I have to be pure in heart too!" However, the internalization of purity in the message of Jesus did not involve the imposition of an even heavier demand but a radical subversion of the existing social system. True purity is a matter not of external boundaries and observance but of the heart.

The critique of the purity system is the theme of one of Jesus' most familiar parables, the story of the Good Samaritan.[31] Most often interpreted as a message about being a helpful neighbor, it in fact had a much more pointed meaning in the first-century Jewish social world. It was a critique of a way of life ordered around purity. The key to seeing this is to recognize the purity issues in the story: the priest and Levite were obligated to maintain a certain level of purity; contact with death was a source of major impurity; and the wounded man is described as "half-dead," suggesting that one couldn't tell whether he was dead without coming close enough to incur impurity if he was. Thus the priest and Levite passed by out of observance of the purity laws. The Samaritan (who, not incidentally, was radically impure according to the purity system), on the other hand, is described as the one who acted "compassionately." Thus this beloved and often domesticated parable was originally a pointed attack on the purity system and an advocacy of another way: compassion.

We see the challenge to the purity system not only in Jesus' teaching but in many of his activities. The stories of his healings shatter the purity boundaries of his social world. He touched lepers and hemorrhaging women. He entered a graveyard inhabited by a man with a "legion" of unclean spirits who lived in the vicinity of pigs, which were of course unclean animals.[32] In the last week of his life, according to the synoptic gospels, he brought his challenge to the center of the purity system—the temple—with his action of driving out the money changers and the sellers of sacrificial animals. His charge that the temple authorities had turned the temple into a "den of robbers" may very well refer to the economic interest that the temple elites had in the purity system.

One of his most characteristic activities was an open and inclusive table. "Table fellowship"—sharing a meal with somebody—had a significance in Jesus' social world that is difficult for us to imagine. It was not a casual act, as it can be in the modern world. In a general way, sharing a meal represented mutual acceptance. More specifically, rules surrounding meals were deeply embedded in the purity system. Those rules governed not only what might be eaten and how it should be prepared, but also with whom one might eat. Refusing to share a meal was a form of social ostracism. Pharisees (and others) would not eat with somebody who was impure, and no decent person would share a meal with an outcast. The meal was a microcosm of the social system, table fellowship an embodiment of social vision.

The meal practice of Jesus thus had sociopolitical significance. He frequently ate with outcasts, as well as with others. Moreover, it appears that these were often festive meals, as is indicated by a small detail in the gospel accounts: the participants "reclined" at table. Ordinary meals were eaten sitting; at festive meals, one reclined. Reclining turns a meal into a banquet, a celebration.

His practice of "open commensality"[33] incited criticism from the advocates of the purity system; this criticism has been preserved in the gospels in a number of places. Jesus is accused of "eating with tax collectors and sinners" and is charged with being "a glutton and a drunkard, a friend of tax collectors and sinners." As already noted, tax collectors were among the worst of the untouchables, and *sinners* should be given the meaning it had within a purity system: impure people, "dirty" people.[34]

The open table fellowship of Jesus was thus perceived as a challenge to the purity system. And it was: the meals of Jesus embodied his alternative vision of an inclusive community. The ethos of compassion led to an inclusive table fellowship, just as the ethos of purity led to a closed table fellowship.

Ultimately, the meals of Jesus are the ancestor of the Christian eucharist. The centrality of meals in the early Christian movement and throughout Christian history goes back to the table fellowship of Jesus.[35] In the Christian tradition, of course, the meal has become a ritualized sacred meal, no longer a real meal. But for Jesus, these were real meals with real outcasts. Recognizing this adds a fresh nuance to the eucharist.

The inclusive vision incarnated in Jesus' table fellowship is reflected in the shape of the Jesus movement itself. It was an inclusive movement, negating the boundaries of the purity system. It included women, untouchables, the poor, the maimed, and the marginalized, as well as some people of stature who found his vision attractive. It is difficult for us who live in a world in which we take for granted an attitude (at least as an ideal) of nondiscrimination to appreciate the radical character of this inclusiveness. It is only what we would expect from a reasonably decent person. But in a society ordered by a purity system, the inclusiveness of Jesus' movement embodied a radically alternative social vision.

We can see this by looking at one example: the role of women in the movement. Both official and folk Judaism were deeply androcentric and patriarchal, as were other cultures of the first-century Mediterranean world. Within the Jewish social world, women were nobodies. Though there were alternative voices within Judaism,[36] the dominant voice disenfranchised women. They had few of the rights of men. They could not, for example, be witnesses in a court of law or initiate a divorce. They were not to be taught the Torah (perhaps because the ability to interpret Torah was considered a form of power). They were radically separated from men in public life, almost invisible, as they are still in some traditional parts of the Middle East. Respectable women did not go out of the house unescorted by a family member; adult women were to be veiled in public. Meals outside of the family were always male-only affairs (and if women were present at such meals, they were perceived as courtesans.) A woman's identity was in her father or husband. Women were the victims of male projections; their association with impurity has already been noted.

In this setting, the role of women in the Jesus movement is striking. The stories of Jesus' interactions with women are remarkable.[37] They range from his defense of the woman who outraged an all-male banquet not only by entering it but also by (unveiled and with hair unbraided) washing his feet with her hair, to his being hosted by Mary and Martha and affirming Mary's role as disciple, to his learning from a Syro-Phoenician Gentile woman.[38] Women were apparently part of the itinerant group traveling with Jesus. Indeed, they were apparently among his most devoted followers, as the stories of their presence at his death suggest. The movement itself was financially supported by some wealthy women. Moreover, the evidence is compelling that women played leadership roles in the post-Easter community.

This is not to make the case that Jesus was a feminist; that would be an anachronism. But it does point to the radical social reality constituted by the Jesus movement in first-century Palestine. Within the movement itself, the sharp boundaries of the social world were subverted and an alternative vision affirmed and embodied. It was a "discipleship of equals" embodying "the egalitarian praxis" of Jesus' vision.[39]

The inclusiveness of the Jesus movement continued into the early Christian movement as we hear it described in other parts of the New Testament. It was one of the most striking qualities of the movement. We see it in the book of Acts in the story of the Ethiopian eunuch, which revolves around the issue of purity boundaries.[40] Eunuchs were sexually defective, and hence were near the bottom of the purity system. They were excluded from full participation in the religious life of Israel.[41] The eunuch's question to Philip, "What is to prevent me from being baptized?" is really a question about whether the new community he has just heard about will exclude or include him. He is, of course, included. The famous words of Paul also negate the world of purity and cultural boundaries and express the same inclusiveness: "In Christ there is neither Jew nor Gentile, slave nor free, male nor female".[42] Paul is not here announcing an abstract ideal; rather, this verse reflects the new social reality of the movement itself.[43]

In short, there is something boundary shattering about the *imitatio dei* that stood at the center of Jesus' message and activity: "Be compassionate as God is compassionate." Whereas purity divides and excludes, compassion unites and includes. For Jesus, compassion had a radical sociopolitical meaning. In his teaching and table fellowship, and in the shape of his movement, the purity system was subverted and an alternative social vision affirmed. The politics of purity was replaced by a politics of compassion.

SPIRIT, COMPASSION, AND US

The intra-Jewish battle between Jesus and the advocates of the purity system can be seen as a battle over two different ways to interpret Scripture. Both he and his critics stood in the tradition of Israel and sought to be faithful to it. The elites of his day read Scripture in accordance with the paradigm of holiness as purity. Jesus read it in accordance with the paradigm of compassion. Each provided a lens through which the tradition was seen. It was thus a hermeneutical battle, a conflict between two very different ways of interpreting the sacred traditions of Judaism. It was not, of course, the kind of academic hermeneutical argu-

ment that occurs today in scholarly circles. Rather, it was a hermeneutical battle about the shape of a world, and the stakes
were high.

The same hermeneutical struggle goes on in the church
today. In parts of the church there are groups that emphasize
holiness and purity as the Christian way of life, and they draw
their own sharp social boundaries between the righteous and
sinners. It is a sad irony that these groups, many of which are
seeking very earnestly to be faithful to Scripture, end up em-
phasizing those parts of Scripture that Jesus himself challenged
and opposed. An interpretation of Scripture faithful to Jesus and
the early Christian movement sees the Bible through the lens of
compassion, not purity.

To use a specific example, I am convinced that much of the
strongly negative attitude toward homosexuality on the part of
some Christians has arisen because, in addition to whatever
nonreligious homophobic reasons may be involved, homosexuality is seen (often unconsciously) as a purity issue. For these
Christians, there's something "dirty" about it, boundaries are
being crossed, things are being put together that do not belong
together, and so forth. Indeed, homosexuality was a purity issue
in ancient Judaism. The prohibition against it is found in the
purity laws of the book of Leviticus.[44]

It seems to me that the shattering of purity boundaries by
both Jesus and Paul should also apply to the purity code's perception of homosexuality.[45] Homosexual behavior should therefore be evaluated by the same criteria as heterosexual behavior.
It also seems to me that the passage in which Paul negates the
other central polarities of his world also means, "In Christ, there
is neither straight nor gay."[46] Granted, Paul didn't say that, but
the logic of "life in the Spirit" and the ethos of compassion
imply it.[47]

It is not only in the church that the politics of purity remains
alive, but also in our culture as a whole. One could make a very
good case that we have a secularized version of the politics of
purity. Our culture has increasingly maximized the rewards for
culturally valued forms of achievement and maximized the pen-
alties for failing to live up to those same standards, thereby
generating increasingly sharp social boundaries. Moreover, the

notion of purity and impurity is at least implicitly present in attitudes toward the poor and people with AIDS.

Seeing compassion as a social paradigm has a further significance for Christians in late-twentieth-century America. Studies of our culture disclose that it is characterized by a pervasive individualism.[48] Within this framework, compassion has become an individual rather than a political virtue. It is to be enacted by "a thousand points of light" rather than being a paradigm for public policy.

In the midst of our modern culture, it is important for those of us who would be faithful to Jesus to think and speak of a politics of compassion not only within the church but as a paradigm for shaping the political order. A politics of compassion as the paradigm for shaping our national life would produce a social system different in many ways from that generated by our recent history.

I do not know what an alternative politics of compassion would look like in detail, and it is possible for Christians to disagree about the details. But in order not to leave this point completely abstract, I will provide one general detail and one that is more specific. A politics of compassion would generate a more "communitarian" dimension in our political life to balance the excesses generated by the dominant politics of individualism. Such an emphasis could involve a recovery of what Robert Bellah calls the "second voice" of the American tradition—namely, its earlier emphasis upon "covenant" and "civic virtue" as images of community.[49] The issue of community (rather than the maximizing of individualism) would become the primary paradigm for thinking about the political order. To provide a more specific instance: it seems to me that, though Christians might disagree about the best way to implement such a system, a politics of compassion in our time clearly implies universal health care as an immediate goal.

I began this chapter by speaking of there being two focal points to the life of Jesus. Jesus was a person of Spirit and a person of compassion, and the two are related. Their connection is pointed to by the same *imitatio dei* that has played such a central role in this chapter: Spirit is compassionate; therefore, be compassionate. But what led Jesus to speak of God as compassionate? How did he become so convinced of this and so passionate about it?

The most persuasive answer locates that conviction in Jesus' own experience of God. It is implausible to see his perception of God as compassionate and the passionate courage with which he held to it as simply a result of the intellectual activity of studying the tradition, or to assume that based on some other grounds he decided it was a good idea. Rather, it is reasonable to surmise that he spoke of God as compassionate — as "like a womb" — because of his own experience of the Spirit.

Such experiences radically subvert social boundaries and culturally generated distinctions by exposing their artificiality and disclosing the "is-ness" that lies beneath the socially constructed maps of reality we erect.[50] The same connection is implicit in the life of the early Christian movement in the decades after Jesus' death. They were, according to the book of Acts and the letters of Paul, communities in which the Spirit was active and present, and they were egalitarian. In short, there is an intrinsic connection between the boundary-shattering experience of Spirit and the boundary-shattering ethos of compassion. Spirit and compassion go together.

The relationship between Spirit and compassion has one further significance. The spiritual life and the world of the everyday are not split apart in the message and activity of Jesus, as they sometimes have been in the history of the church and the lives of Christians. Rather, for Jesus, the relationship with the Spirit led to compassion in the world of the everyday. So also for his most influential follower, Paul. Paul uses the word *love* where Jesus used the word *compassion*. Thus when Paul, in the great "love chapter" in 1 Corinthians 13, speaks of the greatest of the spiritual gifts as love, he is essentially saying that compassion is the primary fruit of the Spirit.

An image of the Christian life shaped by this image of Jesus would have the same two focal points: a relationship to the Spirit of God, and the embodiment of compassion in the world of the everyday. It is an image of the Christian life that provides both direction and growth. For Jesus and Paul, life in the Spirit begins a deepening process of internal transformation whose central quality is compassion. Indeed, growth in compassion is the sign of growth in the life of the Spirit.

NOTES

1. Luke 6.36. I have three brief comments about this verse. First, it is early tradition; its close parallel in Matthew 5.48 indicates that it was part of Q. Second, Luke's wording ("compassionate") is to be preferred to Matthew ("perfect"); the use of the word *perfect* is a demonstrable characteristic of Matthew's redaction. Finally, along with the New English Bible, the Jerusalem Bible, and the Scholar's Version, I prefer the translation "compassionate" to "merciful" (King James, RSV, and NRSV). *Merciful* in English has connotations quite different from *compassionate*, about which I will say more slightly later in this chapter.

2. I owe this insight and the train of thought that flows from it to the work of Phyllis Trible in her book *God and the Rhetoric of Sexuality* (Philadelphia: Fortress, 1978), especially chaps. 2 and 3.

3. Respectively, 1 Kings 3.26 and Genesis 43.30. See Trible, *God and the Rhetoric of Sexuality,* pp. 31–34.

4. See, for example, 1 Kings 3.26, where Solomon has to decide between the claims of two women to being the mother of the same baby. When Solomon proposes to settle the case by cutting the infant in two, the real mother, we are told, was moved in her womb. Interestingly, though the Hebrew word for "womb" is used, the King James Version reads, ". . . her *bowels* yearned upon her son."

5. One text, though, does speak of a *man's* "womb" being moved: Genesis 43.30.

6. See, for example, Exodus 34.6; 2 Chronicles 30.9; Nehemiah 9.17, 31; Psalms 103.8; Joel 2.13; John 4.2.

7. For example, Psalms 25.6, 40.11, 51.1, 69.16, 77.9, 79.8, 103.4, 119.77, 145.9.

8. Jeremiah 31.20. The translation is from Trible, *God and the Rhetoric of Sexuality,* pp. 45, 50; with exegesis on pp. 40–50.

9. In my quotation of Luke 6.36 in the second paragraph of this chapter, I have used the gender-inclusive word *God* instead of *Father,* which is used in the Greek text: "Be compassionate as your Father is compassionate." The juxtaposition of "Father" and "like a womb" is interesting, and provides material for speculation. One might imagine Jesus saying, "You want to know what your heavenly Father is like? Your heavenly Father is like a womb." We perhaps should imagine him saying it with a wink. Such playful yet serious use of language is characteristic of the Jesus tradition.

10. Leviticus 19.2.

11. I am using *politics* here in a broad sense to mean (as its Greek root suggests) concern with the shape and shaping of "the city" (Greek *polis* means "city") and, by extension, concern with the shape and shaping of any human community.

12. Leviticus 19.2. The "holiness code," which defines holiness as purity, is found in Leviticus 17–26. The purity laws collected in Leviticus 11–16 were also important, as are other purity laws scattered throughout the Pentateuch.

13. Jerome Neyrey, *The Social World of Luke-Acts* (Peabody, MA: Hendrickson, 1991), p. 275. Neyrey provides one of the clearest and most accessible expositions of the purity system of Jewish Palestine; see pp. 271–304 of the volume just cited, and his "The Idea of Purity in Mark's Gospel" in *Semeia* 35, ed. John H. Elliott (Decatur, GA: Scholars Press, 1986), pp. 91–128. See also William Countryman, *Dirt, Greed, and Sex* (Philadelphia: Fortress, 1988), especially pp. 11–65. Countryman focuses his lucid exposition on the relationship between the purity system and sexual ethics.

14. There are both broad and somewhat narrower definitions of what constitutes a purity system. Mary Douglas, an anthropologist whose work has been influential in New Testament scholarship, defines a purity system very broadly as an orderly cultural system of classification, lines and boundaries, which makes the terms *purity system* and *culture* virtually synonymous. See her *Purity and Danger: An Analysis of Concepts of Pollution and Taboo* (London: Routledge and Kegan Paul, 1966). Somewhat more narrowly, a purity system may be understood as a cultural system of classification that makes explicit use of the language of purity. The social world of Jesus was a purity system not just in the broad sense, but also in this narrower sense.

15. Cited in Neyrey, *Social World of Luke-Acts*, p. 279.

16. The way in which the purity system worked is quite complex, and a detailed description is beyond the scope of this book. It should be noted, however, that some violations of the purity laws were routine and their consequences short-lived and thus, in a sense, not serious; that is, such violations were taken care of by the passage of time and/or simple rituals. For example, an emission of semen rendered a man unclean until the next day. But regular nonobservance of the purity laws rendered one chronically unclean.

17. I say "perhaps" because the lists that mention shepherds as belonging to the "most despised" category by virtue of their occupations

are found in Jewish sources written down after the time of Jesus. For the lists, see Joachim Jeremias, *Jerusalem in the Time of Jesus* (London: SCM, 1969), p. 304. For a balanced treatment of whether shepherds were outcasts in the first century, see Richard A. Horsley, *The Liberation of Christmas: The Infancy Narratives in Social Context* (New York: Crossroad, 1989), pp. 102–6; Horsley concludes that shepherds were in any case from the peasant class and thus marginals.

18. I believe it was Krister Stendahl, a New Testament scholar who was dean of Harvard Divinity School before becoming a bishop of the Church of Sweden, who said, in a talk I heard some twenty-five years ago about the theological belief that Christians are all sinners, "Of course, we are only honorary sinners."

19. As E. P. Sanders argues in *Jesus and Judaism* (Philadelphia: Fortress, 1985), p. 210, *sinners* could refer to the notoriously wicked. But it was also used by various groups within Judaism to refer to other Jews who were not observant according to the standards of that group. See the very helpful essay by James D. G. Dunn, "Pharisees, Sinners, and Jesus," in *The Social World of Formative Christianity and Judaism*, ed. Jacob Neusner et al. (Philadelphia: Fortress, 1988), pp. 264–89 (especially pp. 276–80).

20. An important clarification: so far as I know, there are no purity sayings that explicitly associate wealth with purity and poverty with impurity. But a purity system is more than the sum of a culture's explicit purity laws. Purity systems have a logic and structure that cause notions of pure and impure to become associated with other central contrasts in the society.

21. See, for example, Countryman, *Dirt, Greed, and Sex*, pp. 28–30; after examining texts from the Pentateuch, he concludes, "It is not too much to suggest that the texts demonstrate a general anxiety about the polluting potential of women."

22. See the purity map in Neyrey, *The Social World of Luke-Acts*, pp. 278–79, which consists of ten concentric circles of decreasing degrees of holiness/purity radiating out from the temple in Jerusalem. At its center is the most sacred part of the temple, the holy of holies; the outermost circle is the land of Israel itself, which is "holy" (and this is one of the meanings of *the holy land:* it is pure and is to be kept pure). Beyond Israel all is "impure"—that is, "off the purity map."

23. In addition to the tithes paid to the temple and priesthood, Jewish farmers were also subject to taxes by Herodian (in Galilee) and Roman (in Judea) authority. We do not know if the payment of tithes

consistently involved the threat of physical coercion, though it sometimes did. There were, in any case, forms of social and economic coercion. Nonobservant Jews (including non-tithe payers) were socially ostracized by those committed to purity; and the classification of untithed produce as impure, and therefore not to be bought by the observant, amounted to an economic boycott. It is hard to know how effective this boycott was. But it could have been significant. If we assume that most of the wealthy aristocracy—generally large landowners—were committed to purity (as they probably would have been, given that the high priestly families were at the center of the aristocracy), it is possible to imagine them refusing to buy produce from their sharecroppers unless the tithes were first paid.

24. The quest for the historical Pharisees has yielded almost as much diversity as the quest for the historical Jesus. The common negative portrait of them in many Christian circles, and their image in popular language as "hypocrites" (and worse), are certainly wrong. They were in fact devout. However, there is considerable scholarly disagreement about who they were in the time of Jesus, the extent of their influence and activity, and so forth. For what seems to me to be a balanced, compact sorting through of the scholarly debate, see Dunn, "Pharisees, Sinners, and Jesus."

25. For "state of research" treatments, see the popular-level book by Hershel Shanks et al., *The Dead Sea Scrolls After Forty Years* (Washington, DC: Biblical Archaeology Society, 1991), and the more scholarly *Understanding the Dead Sea Scrolls,* ed. Hershel Shanks (New York: Random House, 1992). For a compact discussion questioning the identification of Qumran, the Dead Sea Scrolls, and the Essenes, see Norman Golb, "The Qumran-Essene Hypothesis: A Fiction of Scholarship," *Christian Century,* 9 Dec. 1992, pp. 1138–43.

26. Two prominent contemporary scholars disagree about the extent to which Jews observed the purity laws. Jacob Neusner, the most important Jewish scholar of this period, thinks that "ordinary Jews" did not observe them; E. P. Sanders, who has written extensively about Judaism in this period, thinks they did. See Sanders, *Judaism: Practice and Belief, 63 B.C.E.–66 C.E.* (Philadelphia: Trinity Press International, 1992), p. 229.

27. Luke 11.42 = Matthew 23.23, and therefore Q material (and thus quite early tradition). The passage ends with "these you ought to have done, without neglecting the others." The concluding phrase may indicate that Jesus approved of tithing and simply lamented the

neglect of weightier matters such as justice; or the phrase could conceivably be understood ironically.

28. Luke 11.44, with a "fractured" parallel in Matthew 23.27.

29. Mark 7.15.

30. Matthew 5.8. See also Matthew 23.25–26 = Luke 11.39–41. About Matthew 5.8, we cannot be confident that Jesus said this. The words are found only in Matthew, and in a setting where it looks like they might have been "constructed" to fit the context (the Beatitudes of the Sermon on the Mount). Yet it so clearly coheres with authentic sayings of Jesus that one can say that it expresses the gist of what he said about purity, even if he didn't say those exact words.

31. Luke 10.29–37.

32. Mark 5.1–20. In its present form, the story contains many symbolic elements, so it is difficult to discern the extent to which a historical event lies behind it. The point, however, is that the story in its present form shatters the symbolic universe of the purity system.

33. The phrase is from John Dominic Crossan's recent and very important scholarly book on Jesus, *The Historical Jesus: The Life of a Mediterranean Jewish Peasant* (San Francisco: HarperSanFrancisco, 1991). Crossan finds "open commensality" to be one of the two most radical aspects of Jesus' activity; the other is "free healing," which provided access to divine power outside of established religious authority.

34. The use of "dirty" here should not, of course, be understood in the sense of physical dirtiness (though some of Jesus' table companions were in all likelihood physically dirty). Rather, it has the meaning it has within a purity system.

35. And Jesus' table fellowship does not simply go back to "the last supper." We do not know if Jesus in fact held a "last supper" with his disciples at which elements of the meal (bread and wine) were invested with special significance. The stories of a last supper in the gospels may be the product of the early community's embryonic ritualization of the meal tradition rather than a historical recollection of the last night of Jesus' life. There seems, in this instance, no way of moving beyond "not knowing."

36. Elisabeth Schüssler Fiorenza, *In Memory of Her* (New York: Crossroad, 1985), pp. 106–10, 115–18.

37. See the comment in Walter Wink, *Engaging the Powers* (Minneapolis: Fortress, 1992), p. 129: "In every single encounter with women in

the four Gospels, Jesus violated the mores of his time"; for Wink's extended treatment of the point, see pp. 129–34. The whole of his chapter on "the domination system" of first-century Jewish Palestine and Jesus' response to it (pp. 109–37) is consistent with the claims I develop in this chapter.

38. Luke 7.36–50, 10.38–42; Mark 7.24–30.

39. The quoted phrases are used frequently in Schüssler Fiorenza, *In Memory of Her.*

40. Acts 8.26–40.

41. See, for example, Deuteronomy 23.1. The eunuch in the story in Acts is also a Gentile, and thus outside of the Jewish purity system. But the point remains: as a eunuch, he could not become a convert to Judaism.

42. Galatians 3.28.

43. It is important to note that, in the judgment of most scholars, Paul did not write the Pastoral Epistles (1 and 2 Timothy, and Titus), which reflect a much different attitude toward women, especially in the classic "proof text" cited by people opposed to the ordination of women: 1 Timothy 2.8–15. By the time the pastorals were written (early second century), conventional patriarchal attitudes toward women were coming back into the movement. Though the author of the pastorals is often spoken of as a second- or third-generation *follower* of Paul, he may in fact have been seeking to *subvert* Paul's radicalism. And when the subversive is subverted, we are back to the conventional.

44. It often surprises people to learn how little the laws of the Old Testament say about homosexuality. The prohibition is stated in Leviticus 18.22, and the penalty specified in Leviticus 20.13.

45. See especially Countryman, *Dirt, Greed, and Sex.* Countryman argues that homosexuality was a purity issue within Judaism, and that the New Testament's internalization of purity negates what the purity code says about homosexuality. I find the logic of this argument persuasive.

46. The reference is to Galatians 3.28, cited earlier.

47. In addition to Countryman, *Dirt, Greed, and Sex,* see Robin Scroggs, *The New Testament and Homosexuality* (Philadelphia: Fortress, 1983). Two "evangelical" books with an understanding of scriptural authority that is close to fundamentalist, but which nevertheless make a case for the compatibility of homosexuality and Christianity,

are Sylvia Pennington, *Good News for Modern Gays*, and Letha Scanzoni and Virginia Mollenkott, *Is the Homosexual My Neighbor?* (San Francisco: Harper & Row, 1980). Among articles on this topic, see John J. McNeil, "Homosexuality: Challenging the Church to Grow," *Christian Century*, 11 Mar. 1987, pp. 242–46.

48. See especially Robert Bellah et al., *Habits of the Heart* (Berkeley: Univ. of California Press, 1985). Based on an extensive study of middle-class Americans, it argues that the dominant element in the American ethos is individualism, affecting everything from love and marriage to work, from politics and justice to religion. See also the sequel by Bellah et al., *The Good Society* (New York: Alfred A. Knopf, 1991).

49. See Bellah et al., *Habits of the Heart* and *The Good Society*.

50. By "is-ness," I seek to express a difficult but obvious notion: namely, that which "is" independently of the maps that we create with language and systems of ordering. Chief among these creations are *social maps* based on culturally generated distinctions. These maps become the source of identity, creating social differentiation and social boundaries. But all of these maps are artificial constructions imposed upon what "is" and what we "are." Beneath the world we construct with language is *is-ness*.

4

Jesus and Wisdom

TEACHER OF ALTERNATIVE WISDOM

Wisdom is one of the most important concepts for an understanding of what the New Testament says about Jesus. It is central for two reasons. On the one hand, Jesus was a teacher of wisdom. This is the strongest consensus among today's Jesus scholars. Whatever else can be said about the pre-Easter Jesus, he was a teacher of wisdom—a *sage*, as teachers of wisdom are called.[1] On the other hand, the New Testament also presents Jesus as the embodiment or incarnation of divine wisdom. In this chapter we shall look at Jesus as a teacher of wisdom, and in the next we shall look at him as "the wisdom of God."

The subject matter of wisdom is broad. Basically, wisdom concerns how to live. It speaks of the nature of reality and how to live one's life in accord with reality. Central to it is the notion of a way or a path, indeed of two ways or paths: the wise way and the foolish way. Teachers of wisdom speak of these two ways, commending the one and warning of the consequences of following the other.

There are two types of wisdom and two types of sages. The most common type of wisdom is conventional wisdom; its teachers are conventional sages. This is the mainstream wisdom of a culture, "what everybody knows," a culture's understandings about what is real and how to live. About this we shall say more later.

The second type is a subversive and alternative wisdom. This wisdom questions and undermines conventional wisdom and speaks of another way, another path. Its teachers are subversive sages, and they include some of the most famous figures of religious history. Within Eastern religions, the two best-known teachers of a world-subverting wisdom are Lao-tzu and the Buddha.[2] Lao-tzu spoke of following a "way" that led away from conventional perceptions and values and toward living in accord with "the Tao" itself. At the center of the Buddha's teaching is the image of a way, "the eightfold path," leading from the world of convention and its "grasping" to enlightenment and compassion. At the fountainhead of the Western philosophical tradition, Socrates taught a subversive wisdom that involved the citizens of Athens in a critical examination of the conventions that shaped their lives. For his efforts, he was executed.[3]

The wisdom of subversive sages is the wisdom of "the road less traveled."[4] And so it was with Jesus: his wisdom spoke of "the narrow way," which led to life, and subverted the "broad way" followed by the many, which led to destruction.[5] To see the narrow way that Jesus spoke of, his subversive and alternative wisdom, we need to look at both the *how* and the *what* of his wisdom teaching.[6]

THE *HOW* OF JESUS' WISDOM TEACHING: APHORISMS AND PARABLES

The forms of speech most frequently used by Jesus as an oral teacher were aphorisms and parables. Aphorisms are short, memorable sayings, great "one-liners." Parables, of course, are short stories. Together, aphorisms and parables are the bedrock of the Jesus tradition, and they put us most directly in touch with the voice of the pre-Easter Jesus. Strikingly, the most certain thing we know about Jesus is that he was a storyteller and speaker of great one-liners.

The aphorisms and parables of Jesus function in a particular way: they are invitational forms of speech. Jesus used them to invite his hearers to see something they might not otherwise see.

As evocative forms of speech, they tease the imagination into activity, suggest more than they say, and invite a transformation in perception.

The aphorisms of Jesus, of which there are more than a hundred, are arresting crystallizations of insight that invite further insight.[7] "You cannot serve two masters," "You cannot get grapes from a bramble bush," "If a blind person leads a blind person, will they not both fall into a ditch," "Leave the dead to bury the dead," "You strain out a gnat and swallow a camel"—all are short, provocative sayings that mean more than what they say and invite the hearers to see something they otherwise might not see.[8]

To see how the aphorisms worked as oral forms of speech, we must imagine them being said one at a time. For the most part, that is not how they appear in the gospels, where they are typically presented in collections. But we have to imagine them, as part of the oral teaching of Jesus, most often used singly. For an oral teacher to string together many pithy sayings in a row inhibits their function and defeats their purpose.

I first became vividly aware of this while watching a Hollywood movie about Jesus in which Jesus delivered the Sermon on the Mount (a collection of aphorisms covering three chapters of Matthew) as a single discourse.[9] About halfway through this scene (indeed, probably before that), I wanted to shout, "Stop! Stop!" The problem was that there were too many topics, most of them spoken about in an evocative way, and all of them strung together with no spaces in between. It just could not have happened that way; an oral teacher, especially a master of wisdom like Jesus, would not do that. Rather, the sayings individually require being thought about. As provocative sayings meant to lead the hearer to a new perception, they require time for digestion.

Thus we need to imagine them being spoken one at a time.[10] Some may have been spoken all by themselves, with no elaboration, as arresting insights left hanging in the air. Others may have been the subject of a longer teaching, the oral text for an expanded discourse.

We also need to imagine the aphorisms being said many times. No oral teacher—perhaps especially no itinerant teacher—uses a great one-liner only once. Thus their particular contexts in the gospels should not be the sole context in which they are heard. Such contexts may at times provide clues as to the aphorism's application, but it is often more illuminating to imagine each aphorism as a repeated piece of oral teaching in the broader context of the social world of Jesus. Moreover, the realization that the aphorisms were said more than once has a further implication. What we have in the gospels is the memorable core (or gist) of sayings that were repeated many times—the resonant lines that hearers would remember as the heart of longer discourses or dialogues.[11]

To suggest further how they worked, let us return to the list of examples cited earlier. Sometimes it is the content of the one-liner that is fresh and arresting:

Leave the dead to bury the dead.

The saying is striking, enigmatic and evocative. There is a way of life that amounts to living in the land of the dead.[12] It invites reflection: who or what is being called dead? And what would it mean to leave the land of the dead?

The next saying is also fresh in its content:

You strain out a gnat and swallow a camel.[13]

The image is humorous, but with a bite to it as well. Apparently directed at advocates of the purity system, it invites hearers to see a concern with purity as analogous to the foolishness of straining out something small while swallowing something huge. The fact that the camel was an impure animal adds to the irony.

Sometimes the content expresses something that everybody would accept as true, but invites an application of that common-place truth to some situation at hand:

No one can serve two masters.[14]

In the ancient world, everybody knew that it was impossible to be a slave to two masters. The saying would thus elicit immediate agreement. Yet clearly it is meant to apply to something other than literally being a slave. To what does it allude? Who or what are the two masters being spoken of? To what does this apply?

So also the following sayings are truisms but invite reflection about their application:

> Figs are not gathered from thorns, nor are grapes picked from a bramble bush.[15]

Again, Jesus' hearers (and we also) would have to say, "Yes, that's true." But what is this observation true about? For what is it a metaphor? What is its lesson?

> Can a blind person lead a blind person? Will they not both fall into a pit?[16]

Yes, that's what happens. But what is the metaphorical meaning, the application? Jesus' hearers are invited to see that there is a way of leading that amounts to blindness, and those who follow that way will suffer the consequences of blindness. But of what does this blindness consist?

Thus the aphorisms of Jesus are best understood as memorable crystallizations of insight that invite further insight. So also the *parables* of Jesus are invitational, using the form of a story. Like the aphorisms, they need to be thought of as spoken many times; just as no aphorist uses a great one-liner only once, so also no great storyteller tells a great story only once. Thus their gospel contexts describe for us only one "performance" of a story that was told many times.[17]

Some of the parables of Jesus are very short, as brief as aphorisms, with the only difference being that they are narratival. We need to imagine these short parables being spoken as aphorisms, memorable enigmatic sayings complete in themselves:

> The Kingdom of God is like leaven which a woman took and hid in three measures of meal, till it was all leavened.

> The Kingdom of God is like treasure hidden in a field, which a man found and covered up; then in his joy he goes and sells all that he has and buys that field.[18]

But some of the parables are full-fledged stories with considerable plot and character development. One can imagine that, in the course of several tellings, these stories would be told in differing ways and expanded to varying lengths. Indeed, it is helpful to see each of these longer parables in their present form in the gospels as plot summaries of a story told many times. Different parts of the plot could be developed at greater length, depending upon what the occasion called for or permitted. For example, it is easy to imagine the details of the prodigal's life in a far country being developed by a creative storyteller like Jesus, or to imagine expansions at various places in the story of the Good Samaritan. That is, since they were originally oral stories, we should not think of them as the set pieces we have in the gospels, recited virtually word for word.

It is important to see how they worked as oral stories. Whereas aphorisms arrest the mind and imagination with a provocative crystallization of insight, the longer parables work differently. By being good stories, they draw the hearer into the world of the narrative. They then invite the hearer to see something else in the light of what happens in the narratival world.[19] Sometimes the invitation is explicit: "Judge for yourself what is right," and a parable follows, or "What do you think?" and a story follows: "There was a man who had two sons . . ."[20]

But even when not explicit, the invitation is implicit. The appeal is not to the will—not "Do this"—but rather, "Consider seeing it this way." As invitational forms of speech, the parables do not invoke external authority. They do not appeal to divine authority, as do the speech forms of divine lawgivers ("Thus says the Lord, you shall . . .") and inspired prophets ("Hear the word of the Lord . . ."). Rather, their authority rests in themselves— that is, in their ability to involve and affect the imagination. Their voice is invitational rather than imperative.

Thus as a wisdom teacher Jesus used aphorisms and parables to invite his hearers to *see* in a radically new way. The appeal is to the imagination, to that place within us in which reside our images of reality and our images of life itself; the invitation is to a different way of seeing, to different images for shaping our understanding of life. This emphasis upon *seeing* runs throughout his message. There are those who have eyes and yet do not see.[21] There is a blindness that afflicts the sighted. And how one sees makes all the difference, "for the eye is the lamp of the body."[22] How we see determines the path that we walk, the way that we live.

That is the *how* of Jesus as a teacher of wisdom. Now to turn to the *what*, the content of his teaching. Jesus used these invitational and provocative forms of speech—aphorisms and parables—to subvert conventional ways of seeing and living, and to invite his hearers to an alternative way of life. As a teacher of wisdom, Jesus was not primarily a teacher of information (what to believe) or morals (how to behave), but a teacher of a way or path of transformation. A way of transformation from what to what? From a life in the world of conventional wisdom to a life centered in God.

THE PROBLEM: CONVENTIONAL WISDOM

We must first look at the opposite of Jesus' subversive and alternative wisdom—namely, conventional wisdom. Understanding what it is and how it functions provides a very helpful hermeneutical tool for interpreting the message of Jesus (and, more generally, the Christian message as we find it in Paul and in later tradition). It also is illuminating for our own self-understanding.

Conventional wisdom is the dominant consciousness of any culture. It is a culture's most taken-for-granted understandings about the way things are (its worldview, or image of reality) and about the way to live (its ethos, or way of life). It is "what everybody knows"—the world that everybody is socialized into through the process of growing up. It is a culture's social construction of reality and the internalization of that construction within the psyche of the individual. It is thus *encultured consciousness*—that is, consciousness shaped and structured by culture or tradition.

Though its specific content varies from culture to culture, conventional wisdom shares a number of general features across cultures. Not only do these common features further define conventional wisdom, but they illustrate how it functions in our lives. They enable us to see that living in accord with conventional wisdom not only was the dominant consciousness of the first-century Jewish social world, but also is the dominant consciousness in our time and culture.

First, conventional wisdom provides guidance about how to live. It covers everything from highly practical matters such as etiquette to the central values and images of the good life found in a culture. To illustrate initially with the trivial, most of us can remember learning table manners as children. "Don't chew with your mouth open." "Don't take the biggest piece of cake on the plate." "Don't sing at the table." We were taught how to eat soup, and some of us were even given a rhyme to help us remember: "As little ships go out to sea, I dip my spoon away from me."[23] We were told to minimize nonverbal bodily noises, though it was not put exactly that way. These are small matters, of course, but they illustrate how pervasive conventional wisdom is and how early we learned it.

More important, conventional wisdom embodies the central values of a culture—its understanding of what is worthwhile and its images of the good life. In first-century Judaism, this kind of guidance was provided by the Torah and the folk wisdom of the culture, some of which is preserved in the book of Proverbs. Ordinary people learned this way of life not through study, but simply by growing up in the culture, just as we do.

Second, conventional wisdom is intrinsically based upon the dynamic of rewards and punishments. You reap what you sow; follow this way and all will go well; you get what you deserve; the righteous will prosper—these are the constant messages of conventional wisdom. This dynamic is the basis of popular Western notions of a last judgment in which we are rewarded or condemned according to our behavior and/or belief, as well as the basis of popular Eastern notions of karma. It is also found in secular form: work hard and you will succeed. It carries with it a hard-edged corollary, of course: if you don't succeed, or are not blessed, or do not prosper, it is because you have not followed the right path. Life becomes a matter of requirement and reward, failure and punishment.

Third, conventional wisdom has both social and psychological consequences. Socially, it creates a world of hierarchies and boundaries. Some of these may be inherited, as when differences in gender, race, or physical condition are assigned different cultural values and roles. Some are more the product of performance: there are some people who measure up to the standards of conventional wisdom better than others.

Psychologically, conventional wisdom becomes the basis for identity and self-esteem. It is internalized within the psyche as the superego, as "that which stands over me" and to which I must measure up.[24] The superego (whether we choose to call it that or not) is the internalized voice of culture, the storehouse of *ought*s within our heads, and it functions as a generally critical (though sometimes congratulatory) internal voice. It is the internal cop and the internal judge. Conventional wisdom provides its specific content. I am who I am according to the standards of conventional wisdom, and I will think well or poorly of myself depending upon how well I measure up to its standards. Conventional wisdom is thus life under the superego.

In short, whether in religious or secular form, conventional wisdom creates a world in which we live. It constructs a world; indeed, it is the construction. It is a domestication of reality, a net we cast over reality. It is basically life within the socially constructed world.

Life in this world can be and often is grim. It is a life of bondage to the dominant culture, in which we become automatic cultural persons, responding automatically to the dictates of culture. It is a life of limited vision and blindness, in which we see what our culture conditions us to see and pay attention to what our culture says is worth paying attention to. It is a world of judgment: I judge myself and others by how well I and they measure up. It is a world of comparisons: I may be aware that I am not the most attractive person in the world, but because I am more attractive than some, I am "okay." Our identity and self-esteem often depend upon these kinds of comparisons, most of which are quite unconscious but nevertheless very powerful.

It is a life of anxious striving, and feeling okay or not okay to the extent that we do or do not measure up. It is living according to the "performance principle," in which everything depends upon how well I perform.[25] Life according to the performance principle is also life according to the conformity principle: ironically, we try to be outstanding—to *stand out*—by conforming to the standards that our culture values most highly. It is thus also life under the lordship of culture. Finally, it is a life of profound self-preoccupation—with how well we're doing, with our identity, with our security—and thus a life of profound selfishness. Selfishness seldom has to do with reaching for the biggest piece of cake on the plate; rather, it is preoccupation with our selves.

Moreover, this way of being is not unusual but is in fact pervasive. Somewhat startlingly, it reflects normal adult consciousness, both in Jesus' time and in our time. In an important sense, becoming an adult means internalizing the conventional wisdom of one's own culture. It is what faith-development researchers variously call the "conventional-synthetic" stage of life, the stage of "the adult," or the "conformist" stage.[26]

There is an image of God that goes with the world of conventional wisdom. When conventional wisdom appears in religious form, God is imaged primarily as lawgiver and judge. God may be spoken of in other ways as well (for example, as forgiving and gracious), but the bottom line is that God is seen as both the source and enforcer, and therefore the legitimator, of the religious form of conventional wisdom. God becomes the one whom we must satisfy, the one whose requirements must be met.[27]

When this happens in the Christian tradition, it leads to an image of the Christian life as a life of requirements. Indeed, this happens so frequently that it is the most common form of Christianity. It is important to realize this, in part so that we do not make the mistake of equating conventional wisdom with Judaism and alternative wisdom with Christianity. It is very common for Christians (and some scholars) to identify Judaism with a religion of law and an image of God as wrathful and judgmental, in contrast to Christianity, which is seen as a religion of grace, with an image of God as forgiving and loving. There are two things wrong with this identification. First, it is historically inaccurate and radically unfair to Judaism. There were voices of alternative wisdom within Judaism. Indeed, Israel began as "the alternative community of Moses" living by "an alternative consciousness,"[28] which also comes to expression in the classical prophets of ancient Israel and in that portion of the wisdom tradition commonly known as "subversive" or "skeptical" wisdom (Ecclesiastes and Job). Second, it misses my point about conventional wisdom completely. Conventional wisdom is not to be identified with any particular tradition; it is pervasive in all traditions. To emphasize the point once again: the conflict between conventional wisdom and alternative wisdom is not a conflict *between* Judaism and Christianity, but a conflict *within* both traditions.

This awareness is also important for the sake of our own self-understanding as Christians. To illustrate from my own experience, I grew up as a Lutheran, in a tradition that emphasized salvation by grace and not by "works of the law." Indeed, "justification by grace" was the battle cry of the Lutheran Reformation; Luther's own personal and theological struggle had been against "salvation by works." As Lutherans, we all knew that we weren't saved by "works." Rather, we were saved by "grace through faith."

Yet this strong emphasis on grace got transformed into a new system of conventional wisdom, not only in my own mind but, I think, in the minds of many Lutherans, and many Christians generally. The emphasis was placed upon *faith* rather than grace, and faith insidiously became the new requirement. *Faith* (most often understood as *belief*) is what God required, and by a lack of faith/belief one risked the peril of eternal punishment. The requirement of faith brought with it all of the anxiety and self-preoccupation that mark life in the world of conventional wisdom. Was one's faith/belief real enough, strong enough? Thus, for many of us latter-day Lutherans, the system of conventional wisdom remained. Only the content of the requirement had changed—from *good works* to *faith*.

There is another consequence of Christian conventional wisdom. The requirement of faith divides the world up into those who have faith and those who don't, with the implication that God is kindly disposed toward the first group and not so kindly disposed toward the second. This understanding is reflected in a popular Christian bumper sticker that reads: "Christians aren't perfect—they're just forgiven." It implies that other people aren't forgiven, and that Christians have done something (become Christian? believed?) that merits forgiveness. There is a smugness and divisiveness in the statement that comes out of the marriage between conventional wisdom and Christianity.

If even the Lutheran tradition, which speaks so emphatically of grace, can so easily become a system of requirement and reward, then it can happen anywhere. From talking with other Christians, I know that my experience is not idiosyncratic. Most report having heard the Christian message as a message of requirements (whether of belief or of behavior or, most often, of both) and of rewards, typically in "the next world," and sometimes in this world as well. Thus Jesus' subversion of conventional wisdom is a subversion not only of the central convictions of his social world, but of many common forms of Christianity as well.

THE *WHAT* OF JESUS' WISDOM TEACHING: SUBVERSIVE AND ALTERNATIVE WISDOM

As a teacher of wisdom, Jesus undermined the world of conventional wisdom and spoke of an alternative. The two are intrinsically linked: the first must be deconstructed in order for the second to appear. Jesus set about this task in a number of ways.

Paradox and Reversal

Jesus often used the language of paradox and reversal to shatter the conventional wisdom of his time. Impossible combinations abound in his teaching. What kind of world is it in which a Samaritan—a heretic and impure person—can be "good," indeed be the hero of a story? What kind of world is it in which a Pharisee—typically viewed as righteous and pure—can be pronounced unrighteous and an outcast can be accepted? What kind of world is it in which riding a donkey can be a symbol of kingship, in which purity is a matter of the heart and not of external boundaries, in which the poor are blessed, the first are last and the last first, the humble exalted and the exalted humbled?

So also Jesus frequently spoke of the Kingdom of God in the language of impossible or unexpected combinations.[29] The Kingdom, something great, is compared to something very tiny: it is like "a grain of mustard seed."[30] Moreover, mustard was a weed; thus, the Kingdom is like a weed. The Kingdom is compared to something impure: it is like a woman (associated with impurity) putting leaven (which was impure) into flour.[31] The Kingdom is for children, who in that world were nobodies: thus, the Kingdom is for nobodies.[32] The same point is made by Jesus' meals with outcasts: the Kingdom is a banquet of outcasts, of nobodies. Many who expect to be in the Kingdom will not be: many shall come from the east and the west to the banquet of the Kingdom, and many of those who expect to be in the Kingdom will find themselves shut out.[33] Moreover, the Kingdom is not somewhere else; rather it is among you, inside you, and outside you. Neither is it some time in the future, for it is here, spread out on the earth; people just do not see it.[34]

Conventional Wisdom as the Broad Way

Like most sages, Jesus spoke of two ways, a wise way and a foolish way, a way of life and a way of death, a narrow way and a broad way:

> Enter by the narrow gate; for the gate is wide and the way is easy that leads to destruction, and those who enter by it are many. For the gate is narrow and the way is hard that leads to life, and those who find it are few.[35]

For most sages, the wise way was the way of conventional wisdom, and the foolish way was the path of disregarding conventional wisdom. Jesus reversed this: he spoke of the broad way that led to destruction not as gross wickedness or flagrant foolishness, but as the way of conventional wisdom. He directly attacked the central values of his social world's conventional wisdom: family, wealth, honor, purity, and religiosity. All were sanctified by tradition, and their importance was part of the taken-for-granted world.

It was against these values that some of his most radical sayings were directed. In that culture, the family (which was patriarchal) was the primary social unit, the center of both identity and material security, and a "good" family was one of the blessings of God. Yet Jesus spoke of leaving family and even of "hating" family.[36] Indeed, his words "Call no man on earth your father, for you have one Father, who is in heaven" may very well be directed against the patriarchal family, which as the primary social unit in that world was a microcosm of a hierarchical system. If so, this is a fascinating instance of Jesus using the image of God as Father in a way that subverted patriarchy.[37]

Far from seeing wealth as a blessing from God for having lived wisely, Jesus saw it as preoccupation and idolatry: "You cannot serve God and mammon."[38] He told stories of people whose preoccupation with possessions caused them to miss the banquet to which they had been invited, of a farmer who spent his life gathering his goods into barns and then died before he really began to live, of a rich man who day after day ignored the beggar at his gate.[39] "It is easier for a camel to go through the eye of a needle than for a rich man to enter the Kingdom of God," he said.[40] Similarly, he ridiculed those who were concerned with honor, castigated concern for purity, and indicted those who trusted in their own religiosity. No wonder those who were secure in the world of conventional wisdom found little worthwhile in his message, and much that was nonsensical, offensive, and threatening.

Jesus' Image of God

In many of his parables and aphorisms, Jesus invited his hearers to see God not as the judge, not as the one who has requirements that must be met, not as the legitimator of conventional wisdom—but as gracious and compassionate. To recall some of the most familiar sayings of Jesus:

> Consider the birds of the air—they neither sow nor reap, they have neither storehouse nor barn, and yet God feeds them.

> Consider the lilies of the field, how they grow; they neither toil nor spin, yet I tell you, even Solomon in all his glory was not arrayed like one of these.[41]

When I was young, I tended to hear these sayings in a judgmental mode, feeling them as an indictment of my insufficiently strong faith: "Oh my God, I don't really trust that much." But now I hear them very differently. Rather than an indictment, they are an invitation to see reality as characterized by a cosmic generosity and by an overflowing effulgence of life. Yet there is nothing of Pollyanna in them, for in the very next line Jesus speaks of the lilies of the field today being beautiful and tomorrow being thrown into the oven:

> But if God so clothes the grass of the field, which today is alive and tomorrow is thrown into the oven, how much more will he clothe you?[42]

The image Jesus evokes recognizes the transitoriness of life, and yet invites us to see the source of all life as gracious and generous.

The same note is sounded in other familiar sayings. Jesus speaks of God as one who makes "the sun to rise on the evil and the good" and as one who "sends the rain upon the just and unjust," without thought of reward or punishment.[43] God knows us well: even the hairs on our heads are numbered. God sees even a sparrow fall—and we are of greater value than many sparrows.[44] In the story of the vineyard owner who pays all of the workers the same amount regardless of how long or how hard they have worked, the hearers are invited to enter a world in which everybody receives what they need.[45] The workers who complain are the voice of the old world, the world of conventional wisdom, and the vineyard owner's response to them is striking: "Do you begrudge my generosity?" The parable invites the hearers to consider that God is like this, and not like the God of requirements and reward.

These themes run through Jesus' best-known story. In the parable of the Prodigal Son, rightly regarded as a masterpiece, we see much: Jesus' artistry as a storyteller, his invitational style, his subversion of conventional wisdom, and the ground of his alternative wisdom—namely, an image of God as gracious and compassionate.

It is useful to think of the form in which we find this story in Luke's gospel as a plot summary of an oral story having three acts, each of which, as mentioned earlier, could be expanded at will.[46] In act one, the prodigal's life is described in considerable detail. It is a picture of going into exile and becoming an outcast. He journeys to a far country (a Gentile country, and therefore an impure land), and there he not only squanders his money on loose living but, reduced to poverty, becomes an employee of a Gentile pig farmer. As a swineherd, he has become (if such is possible) worse than an untouchable. It is difficult to imagine a more abject picture of dereliction in a first-century Jewish context. Act one ends with the prodigal's decision to return home.

In act two, the focus is upon the father. Seeing his son at a great distance, he (significantly) "has compassion" and rushes out to meet him. Before the prodigal can even speak, the father embraces and kisses him. Brushing aside his son's carefully prepared confession, the father joyfully clothes his son with his best robe and puts a ring on his hand and shoes on his feet—all symbols of acceptance and restoration. Then he orders that a banquet be prepared.

The parable could have ended here, and it would have been a powerful statement about the compassion of God and the acceptance of the untouchables. But it doesn't. In act three, which begins with the sound of music and dancing floating into the nearby fields, the focus shifts to yet a third character, the older son. Hearing the sounds of celebration and finding out what is going on from a servant, he adamantly refuses to join the banquet. Instead, he complains: all these years he has been a dutiful and obedient son, and he was never so wondrously treated. The father implores him to join the celebration, and the parable ends with a question hanging in the air: will the older son's sense of the way things ought to be keep him out of the banquet?[47]

The parable represents a systematic subversion of the world of conventional wisdom. The elder son's voice is the voice of conventional wisdom itself; it is his voice that the hearers are invited to hear as perhaps their own—and then to reject. It is not necessary to turn the parable into an allegory to see that the character of the father is like God—compassionate, yearning for his son lost in exile, rejoicing at his return. Moreover, the story of the prodigal images the religious life very differently from how it is seen within the world of conventional wisdom: as a life of exile "in a far country" and a journey of return—not as a life of duty, requirements, and rewards. Between the two there is an enormous gap.

Thus the image of God at the center of Jesus' teaching undermines the dynamic of requirements and rewards at the core of conventional wisdom. To speak of God as gracious and compassionate—as *womblike*, to recall a theme from the previous chapter—is very different from imaging God as the lawgiver and judge enforcing the life of requirements. Indeed, if we take the graciousness of God seriously, it completely undermines the world of conventional wisdom, whether in religious or secular form.

This emphasis upon the graciousness of God in the message of Jesus often leads to questions about whether there is any element of judgment at all. A number of clarifying remarks may help. The passages in the synoptics that speak of a last judgment with eternal consequences are largely the products of Matthew's redaction. Moreover, the notion that our life on earth is primarily about meeting God's requirements so that we may have a blessed *next* life is, it seems to me, foreign to Jesus. Though I think he probably "believed in an afterlife,"[48] I don't think his message was about how to get there.

In the few texts where he does speak of a last judgment, it is to subvert widely accepted notions about that judgment.[49] In short, it seems that the threat of being judged by God for one's sins at the last judgment was not central to Jesus, if it was in his message at all. Yet the notion of *historical* judgment does play a role in Jesus' message, in much the same way as it does in the classical prophets of the Old Testament: blindness has its consequences, both for a society and for the individual. On the level of society, because Jerusalem (the center of the ruling elites) did not know "the things that make for peace," historical conflict lay ahead.[50] On the individual level (now as then), if one does not leave the world of conventional wisdom, one remains in it, living in "the land of the dead." That (and not the threat of hell) is the issue.

THE WAY LESS TRAVELED

What then is the way that leads to life? The narrow way, the way less traveled, is the alternative wisdom of Jesus. It has two closely related dimensions. First, it is an invitation to see God as gracious and womblike rather than as the source and enforcer of the requirements, boundaries, and divisions of conventional wisdom (whether Jewish, Christian, or secular). Second, it is an invitation to a path that leads away from the life of conventional wisdom to a life that is more and more centered in God. The alternative wisdom of Jesus sees the religious life as a deepening relationship with the Spirit of God, not as a life of requirements and reward.

What that path involves is suggested by a number of images. Jesus used imagery of the heart to speak of the need for an internal transformation. For Jesus, as for ancient Jewish psychology generally, the heart represented the self at its deepest level. When the heart is centered in the finite, it becomes closed and hardened rather than open and receptive. What is needed, then, is a new heart—an internal transformation brought about by a deep centering in God.

Here the thoroughgoing monotheism of Jesus (and of Judaism itself) can be most clearly seen: "You shall love the Lord your God with all your heart, soul, and mind."[51] This is the essence of the narrow way of Jesus. Indeed, one can see his alternative wisdom as a radicalization of the first commandment, which set it over against the conventions of tradition, even the conventions of sacred tradition. For it is possible to be centered in sacred tradition and yet have one's heart far from God.[52]

The narrow way as the path of internal transformation is also pointed to by a second image. In imagery that the gospel writers emphasize and extend but that also may go back to Jesus himself, the narrow way is spoken of as the way of death: "Whoever does not carry the cross and follow me cannot be my disciple."[53] Death as an image for the path of transformation points to a dying to the world of conventional wisdom as the center of one's security and identity and a dying to the self as the center of one's concern. It is a striking image for the path of spiritual transformation. Not only is death the ultimate *letting go*, and thus the opposite of the *grasping* that marks the life of conventional wisdom, but the process may often involve the stages we have come to associate with the physical process of dying: denial, anger, bargaining, depression, and acceptance. The path of death is also, for Jesus, the path to new life. It results in rebirth, a resurrection to a life centered in God.

Put even more compactly, the way less traveled is life in the Spirit. It is the life that Jesus himself knew. The transformation of perception to which Jesus invited his hearers flowed out of his own spiritual experience. This seems the best explanation of the origin of Jesus' wisdom. There is a sovereign voice in his wisdom, one that knows tradition but whose vantage point is not simply tradition.

We may suppose that the source of this sovereign voice was an enlightenment experience similar to such experiences reported of other great sages.[54] As one who knew God, Jesus knew God as the compassionate one, not as the God of requirements and boundaries. The life to which he invited his hearers was the life in the Spirit that he himself had experienced. The narrow way, the road less traveled, is life centered in the Spirit of God.

It is a challenging message for both secular and Christian forms of conventional wisdom in our time. Our culture's secular wisdom does not affirm the reality of the Spirit; the only reality about which it is certain is the visible world of our ordinary experience. Accordingly, it looks to the material world for satisfaction and meaning. Its dominant values are what I call the three A's—achievement, affluence, and appearance. We live our lives in accord with these values, with both our self-worth and level of satisfaction dependent upon how well we measure up to these cultural messages. Not only is the effort to measure up burdensome, but even when we are reasonably successful at doing so, we often find the rewards unsatisfying. We may have the experience of being satiated and yet still hungry. Perhaps Augustine and others were right when they said that we are made in such a way that we have an appetite for the infinite. The signs that people in modern culture often do yearn for something more are many and encouraging.[55]

The way of Jesus also challenges many common forms of Christianity, as already noted. In particular, it invites us to move from "secondhand religion" to firsthand religion.[56] Secondhand religion is a way of being religious based on believing what one has heard from others. It consists of thinking that the Christian life is about believing what the Bible says or what the doctrines of the church say. Firsthand religion, on the other hand, consists of a relationship to that to which the Bible and the teachings of the church point—namely, that reality that we call God or the Spirit of God.

The transformation from secondhand religion to firsthand religion, from living in accord with what one has heard to life centered in the Spirit, is central to the alternative wisdom of Jesus and also to the Jewish tradition in which he stood. One of the most powerful expressions of this transformation is to be found in the book of Job.[57] At its climax, after Job has experienced a dramatic self-disclosure of God, he exclaims:

> I had heard of thee by the hearing of the ear,
> but now my eye beholds thee.[58]

That change—from having heard about God with the hearing of the ear to "beholding" God, from secondhand belief to firsthand relationship—is what the alternative wisdom of Jesus is most centrally about.

The gospel of Jesus—the good news of Jesus' own message—is that there is a way of being that moves beyond both secular and religious conventional wisdom. The path of transformation of which Jesus spoke leads from a life of requirements and measuring up (whether to culture or to God) to a life of relationship with God. It leads from a life of anxiety to a life of peace and trust. It leads from the bondage of self-preoccupation to the freedom of self-forgetfulness. It leads from life centered in culture to life centered in God.

NOTES

1. The consensus flows out of the convergence of two streams of research over the last twenty years: intensive study of the oral forms of Jesus' teaching (primarily aphorisms and parables, both wisdom forms of speech, about which we shall say much in this chapter); and analyses of the Q tradition, which argue that its early layer is dominated by wisdom forms. Emergent understandings of the Gospel

of Thomas (which, as noted earlier, is seen by many scholars to contain some material as old as anything in the synoptics) corroborate the centrality of wisdom to the Jesus tradition: Thomas, like Q, is a wisdom document. Disagreements among Jesus scholars center not on whether Jesus was a teacher of wisdom, but on whether there are other "strokes" of major importance that should be included in a sketch of Jesus.

2. Lao-tzu (China, sixth century B.C.) is reputedly the author of a collection of relatively short allusive and evocative sayings known as the *Tao Te Ching* (with the *t*'s pronounced as *d*'s); his influence has been important in Zen Buddhism as well as in Taoism itself. The teaching of the Buddha (about a century later in India) subverted the traditional world of the Hindu tradition in important respects; at its center was "the eightfold path" leading away from the world of convention.

3. For the account of Socrates' trial and execution, see Plato's dialogues "Euthyphro," "Apology," "Crito," and "Phaedo," available in many editions. It is striking that Socrates and Jesus, the two most central figures in the philosophical and religious traditions of the West, were both executed. Clearly, challenging conventional wisdom is often experienced as offensive and threatening.

4. Both types of wisdom are found in the Jewish tradition prior to Jesus. The wisdom books of the Hebrew Bible include Proverbs, Ecclesiastes, and Job. Much of Proverbs (especially the collection of sayings in chaps. 10–30) expresses conventional wisdom, whereas the authors of Ecclesiastes and Job are voices of a subversive and alternative wisdom. Thus there is a tension or dialectic within the wisdom tradition itself. Indeed, Ecclesiastes and Job can be understood as a radical questioning of the easy confidence of the conventional wisdom of Proverbs that if one lives right, all will go well. For an excellent, accessible introduction to Jewish wisdom, including an appreciative treatment of Proverbs, see Kathleen M. O'Connor, *The Wisdom Literature* (Wilmington, DE: Michael Glazier, 1988).

5. Matthew 7.13–14.

6. Many of the themes of this chapter are also treated in my book *Jesus: A New Vision* (San Francisco: Harper & Row, 1987), pp. 97–124.

7. The most comprehensive scholarly study of the aphorisms is John Dominic Crossan's *In Fragments: The Aphorisms of Jesus* (San Francisco: Harper & Row, 1983). I have referred to the aphorisms as "great one-liners," even though they are sometimes several lines

long. But even the longer ones (such as "Consider the birds . . . consider the lilies . . ." in Luke 12.22–31 = Matthew 6.25–34) are designed to be memorable as oral speech.

8. Luke 16.13 = Matthew 6.24; Luke 6.44 = Matthew 7.16; Luke 6.39 = Matthew 15.14; Luke 9.60 = Matthew 8.22; Matthew 23.24. An aphorism is both like and unlike its nearest relative, the proverb. Both are short, pithy sayings designed to be memorable in an oral culture. A proverb, however, typically expresses *folk wisdom*—the collective and conventional wisdom of the culture itself. An aphorism expresses the fresh vantage point or perspective of a particular individual. Thus the essential contrast is between *collective wisdom* and *individual wisdom*.

9. Matthew 5–7. There is some parallel material in Luke 6.20–49 and other parallel material scattered throughout Luke. This indicates that many of the individual sayings in the Sermon on the Mount are Q material, and that the sermon *as a connected whole* is a construction by Matthew.

10. There are exceptions, of course. One can imagine a number of parallel sayings being spoken on a single occasion (for example, a collection of beatitudes or woes), and one can imagine a longer passage like "Consider the birds . . . consider the lilies . . ." as a connected discourse. But what one cannot imagine is "Consider the birds . . . consider the lilies . . . ," *immediately* followed by "Judge not, that you be not judged," immediately followed by "Why do you see the speck in your brother's eye," immediately followed by "Do not give dogs what is holy," and so forth, as Matthew has it (that is, Matthew 6.25–34 followed by Matthew 7.1ff).

11. The idea that what we have is the gist has two implications. First, it means that we never have direct quotation (or if we do, it is accidental, and we have no way of recognizing it as such). Crossan provides a classic example (*In Fragments*, p. 38): most Americans know the gist of Franklin D. Roosevelt's famous saying about fear. But did he say, "You have nothing to fear but fear itself," or "There is nothing to fear but fear itself," or . . . ? Crossan then lists four other possibilities. The point: we can know the gist without being sure of the exact quotation. Second, we need to be aware that the gist can sometimes be more than simply the memorable core underlying variations of a saying. The gist can also be the *condensation* of a longer discourse, in which case we should think of the saying not as functioning by itself as a single statement left hanging in the air, but as the theme of a more extended teaching.

12. Luke 9.59–60 = Matthew 8.21–22 (and thus Q). In the Q context (which may not be the only context for the saying, and perhaps not even *a* context), the land of the dead is the world of filial obligation: the would-be follower wants time to bury his father, one of the most sacred obligations in Jesus' world.

13. Matthew 23.24.

14. Matthew 6.24 = Luke 16.13.

15. Luke 6.44 = Matthew 7.16.

16. Luke 6.39 = Matthew 15.14.

17. Of the many important scholarly books written on the parables in the last twenty years, Bernard Brandon Scott's *Hear Then the Parable* (Minneapolis: Fortress, 1989) is the most comprehensive.

18. From, respectively, Luke 13.21 = Matthew 13.33; Matthew 13.44.

19. Indeed, the roots of the word *parable* mean "to throw alongside of"; a parable is a story "thrown alongside of" some life situation.

20. Luke 12.57; Matthew 21.28.

21. Mark 8.18.

22. Matthew 6.22–23 = Luke 11.34–35. It is perhaps more common to read this passage as if the eye is the way the *inside* of the body is illuminated, a reading encouraged by the rest of the passage. In this reading, it is as if the eye were a window letting light into the body. My suggested reading, however, interprets the passage by way of analogy to the verse from Ps. 119: "Thy word is a lamp on to my feet." Here the image is of a lamp lighting one's path as one journeys along. To call the eye the lamp of the body is to say that how one sees illuminates one's path.

23. I have since learned that not many people know this rhyme, and I have concluded that it was North Dakota (or perhaps Norwegian-immigrant) "*hoch* etiquette."

24. The term *superego* derives, of course, from Freud. The German term he used is more expressive: *das Über-Ich*—"that which stands over me." Whether one likes Freud or not, it seems to me that the term designates a psychological reality that we are all familiar with: an internal mechanism that praises or punishes us to the extent that we measure up to its standards. For the difference between superego and conscience, see the helpful essay by John W. Glaser, "Conscience and Superego," in John J. Heaney, ed., *Psyche and Spirit*, rev. ed. (New York: Paulist, 1984), pp. 31–49.

25. Robin Scroggs, *Paul for a New Day* (Philadelphia: Fortress, 1977), p. 10.

26. The terms belong, respectively, to James Fowler, Sam Keen, and Elizabeth Liebert. Fowler's understanding of life's stages is found in many works; his *Becoming Adult, Becoming Christian* (San Francisco: Harper & Row, 1984) is especially useful. For Keen and Liebert, see Sam Keen, *The Passionate Life* (San Francisco: Harper & Row, 1983); and Elizabeth Liebert, *Changing Life Patterns: Adult Development in Spiritual Direction* (New York: Paulist, 1992).

27. The Freudian insight that religious traditions commonly identify the superego with the voice of God seems to me to be correct. In cultures or communities that affirm that their basic order comes from God, it is natural for the judging voice of the superego to be identified with God. Freud, however, inadequately appreciated the way in which forms of religion can be culture subverting and superego subverting.

28. The phrases are from Walter Brueggemann, *The Prophetic Imagination* (Philadelphia: Fortress, 1978), chap. 1.

29. There were a variety of understandings of *Kingdom of God* in first-century Judaism, and we do not know whether some were more dominant than others: a this-worldly kingdom to be brought about by a war of revolt against Rome or by direct divine intervention, a completely supernatural kingdom beyond or replacing this world, perhaps even a mystical kingdom. But there was common agreement that the Kingdom of God was something "great" and that it was primarily for "Israel," however that was defined. Israel's visions of the glorious time coming did not necessarily exclude the Gentiles, for some of those visions portray the Gentiles also streaming to Jerusalem. Even in those visions, however, the centrality of Israel remained, of course, for it is to Israel's God and Israel's capital that the world comes.

30. Mark 4.30–31.

31. Matthew 13.33 = Luke 13.20–21.

32. For this understanding of children as "nobodies," see especially John Dominic Crossan, *The Historical Jesus*, pp. 266–69. The tendency to see children as symbols of simple or childlike faith is largely a modern emphasis, the product of Christian defensiveness against the faith-threatening corrosiveness of Enlightenment knowledge.

33. Matthew 8.11–12 = Luke 13.28–30.

34. In writing the last two sentences, I side with those scholars who see the Kingdom primarily as a present reality in the message of Jesus and not as a soon-to-come future reality.

35. Matthew 7.13–14; see also Luke 13.24. Somewhat paradoxically, the narrow way that is here spoken of as "hard" is also "easy"; see Matthew 11.28–30.

36. See Luke 14.26 = Matthew 10.37. Those who see Jesus as a champion of "family values" fail to see the radical edge to his message. It is not that he would be against loving one's family (after all, he spoke of loving one's enemies); rather, his attitude toward family is not univocally affirmative: family can be the problem. It is interesting that, during his public activity, his own family relations were strained. According to Mark 3.21, his family sought to restrain him because they thought he had become insane. See also Mark 3.31–35, where *family* is redefined as "those who do the will of God." It was only after Easter, according to the New Testament, that some of Jesus' own family became part of the movement.

37. Matthew 23.9. I find Elisabeth Schüssler Fiorenza's analysis of this often neglected verse persuasive; see Schüssler Fiorenza, *In Memory of Her* (New York: Crossroad, 1985), pp. 149–51. Just as the lordship of God means that one is to have no other lords, so the fatherhood of God means that one is to have no other fathers.

38. Matthew 6.24 = Luke 16.13.

39. Luke 14.16–24 = Matthew 22.1–10 = Thomas 64; Luke 12.13–21; Luke 16.19–31.

40. Mark 10.25. I have wondered whether the camel was chosen for this saying because it is the animal that is fat with what it has stored up, or whether any large animal could equally well have been substituted (for example, a horse).

41. Matthew 6.26–29 = Luke 12.24–27.

42. Matthew 6.30 = Luke 12.28.

43. Matthew 5.45.

44. Luke 12.6–7 = Matthew 10.29–31.

45. Matthew 20.1–15.

46. Luke 15.11–32. Though this parable is found only in Luke, a virtual consensus of scholarship accepts it as reflecting the voice of Jesus. Luke here provides us with one possible "performance" (probably condensed) of an oral story going back to Jesus.

47. As noted in the previous chapter when I spoke about the open table fellowship of Jesus, banquet imagery is central to the gospels. It is tempting to generalize and to suggest that Jesus saw life as a banquet from which many people exclude themselves because of perceptions

and preoccupations flowing out of their embeddedness in the world of conventional wisdom.

48. I have placed this phrase in quotation marks to signal its vagueness and broad range of meanings. I have no idea if Jesus saw the afterlife as including the survival and awareness of one's personal identity. In Mark 12.18–27, for example, Jesus counters the notion that relationships on earth endure into the next world, but there is no way of knowing whether this should be taken to imply that personal identity does not continue. It is important to note that there is another understanding of the afterlife, one that does not involve an awareness of personal identity. For a very illuminating discussion of these two different ways of imagining the afterlife, see David Ray Griffin and Huston Smith, *Primordial Truth and Postmodern Theology* (Albany: State Univ. of New York Press, 1989), pp. 66–67 (pp. 129–30 are also relevant). To bring the point back to Jesus: I think he probably believed in an afterlife, but I have no clear notion of what it means to say that.

49. See, for example, Luke 10.12 = Matthew 10.15; Luke 10.13–14 = Matthew 11.21–22; Luke 11.31 = Matthew 12.42; Luke 11.32 = Matthew 12.41. Each subverts or reverses what some of Jesus' contemporaries believed about the last judgment by saying that *Gentiles* will do better at the judgment than those to whom Jesus was speaking. It's as if he had said, "You believe in a last judgment? Well, let me tell you—it will be much different from what you think." That is, the point of these sayings is not to *affirm* a last judgment, but to undermine conventional ideas about it.

50. Luke 19.41–44. Passages indicating that Jesus warned of the coming destruction of Jerusalem (the center of the ruling elites) as a *historical* event, in much the same manner as Jeremiah did, are found in the earliest layer of the tradition (Q and Mark), as well as in passages found only in Luke.

51. Mark 12.29–30. This passage is spoken of as the greatest of the commandments. It is a quotation of Deut. 6.5, part of the Shema and seen as the crystallization of ancient Israel's primary obligation to God.

52. Mark 7.6–8.

53. Luke 14.27 = Matthew 10.38; Mark 8.34. Many scholars have suspected the imagery of death to be the post-Easter creation of the community as it reflected about Jesus' own death. This may be the case. Yet death as an image for "the way" is found in both Mark and

Q and is thus, at the very least, very early and may go back to Jesus himself.

54. This point is emphasized by Stephen Mitchell in the introduction to his book *The Gospel According to Jesus* (New York: HarperCollins, 1991). Not many scholars have proposed this, but I find Mitchell's suggestion persuasive.

55. One such sign is the remarkable fact that M. Scott Peck's *The Road Less Traveled*, which articulates an alternative wisdom, has been on the *New York Times*'s best-seller list for over ten years.

56. The phrase "secondhand religion" comes from William James, *The Varieties of Religious Experience*, ed. Martin Marty (New York: Penguin, 1982; originally published in 1902), p. 6.

57. The authorship and date of Job are uncertain, but it was probably written around 500 B.C., soon after the Jewish people's experience of exile in Babylon (587–539 B.C.). Along with Ecclesiastes (perhaps written around 300 B.C.), the book is a voice of subversive wisdom in the wisdom tradition of ancient Israel. Note how the core of the book (the dialogues between Job and his "comforters," occupying chaps. 3–37) is a sustained debate about the theme of requirements and rewards ("the righteous will flourish, the wicked will wither"), which stands at the center of conventional wisdom. The "comforters" are defenders of this notion; Job vehemently attacks it.

58. Job 42.5.

Jesus, the Wisdom of God

SOPHIA BECOME FLESH

The second important role played by wisdom in the early Christian movement's imaging of Jesus is Christological. The early layers of the movement's developing traditions portray Jesus not only as a teacher of wisdom, but also as intimately related to "the wisdom of God." Central voices in the New Testament—Matthew, Luke, Paul, and John—speak of this relationship in various ways, imaging Jesus as the emissary, child, and incarnation of the wisdom of God. Jesus was a wisdom teacher who was also, in some sense, the wisdom of God.

Treating this subject involves us in Christology—the branch of Christian theology that deals with the nature of Christ. Compactly and broadly, Christology focuses on the relationship between Jesus and God. Its subject matter includes the Christological images of the New Testament, the humanity and divinity of Jesus and how the two are related to each other, and the Christological teachings contained in the church's official statements of faith, as formulated by church councils at Nicea (A.D. 325) and Chalcedon (A.D. 451).

The bishops at Nicea produced the Nicene Creed, which has been especially important in shaping Christian images of Jesus, or what might be called (nonpejoratively) popular-level Christology. The threefold division of the creed into sections about Father, Son, and Spirit reflect the emerging Trinitarian dogma of the fourth century. Its structure and content together identify Jesus as "Son of the Father" and the second person of the Trinity. As such, he is the only begotten Son of God, begotten before all worlds, God of God, Light of Light, very God of very God, indeed, "of one substance with the Father."[1]

All of this—the identification of Jesus as the divine Son of God the Father, and the specific phrases used to speak of his status—is very familiar to Christians because of the role of the Nicene Creed in the church ever since. Not only did the creed define orthodoxy, but its recitation in Christian worship services over the centuries deeply ingrained a "Son of God" Christology within the collective Christian psyche, and thereby within the psyche of the West.

As a result, the most familiar Christology to people both within and outside of the church is one that images Jesus' relationship to God as Son of the Father. This Son of God Christology is the core of the popular image of Jesus.[2] So familiar is it that it is easy to think of it as the normative or definitive Christology.

But this had not yet happened in the New Testament period. There was as yet no official Christology. Rather, the New Testament contains a variety of Christological images, which function as metaphors for imaging the significance of Jesus and his relationship to God. They had not yet been crystallized into doctrines, and the language of "substance," "person," and "two natures" was still far in the future. Among these metaphors was the root of what was to become the Son of God Christology of the later church: the New Testament does use son/father imagery to speak about Jesus and God. But along with son/father imagery were other images.[3] One of these, probably as early as and perhaps even earlier than son/father imagery, is an image of Jesus as intimately related to divine wisdom. Developing alongside the early Christian movement's embryonic son/father Christology was an embryonic wisdom Christology that ultimately saw Jesus as the embodiment or incarnation of "the wisdom of God."

Seeing this wisdom Christology can affect our image of Jesus in more than one way. It not only can enrich our imaging of Jesus but also, as we shall see, provides a window into seeing the nature of Christological language.

WISDOM IN THE JEWISH TRADITION

The ingredients of wisdom Christology come from the Jewish tradition. There *wisdom* has a number of meanings. It can refer to a literary genre—namely to the books of wisdom found in the Hebrew Bible (Proverbs, Job, and Ecclesiastes) and in the Apocrypha (Sirach, and Wisdom of Solomon). It can also refer to the collected teachings of sages, "the sayings of the wise," which provided practical counsel for living the wise way.

There is a third meaning as well, and it is this one that is foundational for understanding the early Christian movement's language about Jesus as the wisdom of God. In Jewish wisdom literature, wisdom is often personified in female form as "the Wisdom Woman." Consistent with this personification, *wisdom* is a feminine noun in both Hebrew (*hokmah*) and Greek (*sophia*). Among scholars, it has become common to name this personification *Sophia*, even when the reference is to a Hebrew text. The obvious reason for doing so (besides the fact that Greek texts use *sophia*) is that *Sophia* is a woman's name in English, thereby reminding us of the female personification in a way that the neuter-sounding word *wisdom* does not. Thus, in the biblical texts quoted in this chapter, I use "Sophia" whenever the passage personifies wisdom as a woman.[4]

This personification is first developed in the opening chapters of Proverbs. The Wisdom Woman, Sophia, appears in chapter 1, speaking in a public place like one of the prophets of ancient Israel:

> Sophia cries out in the street; in the squares she raises her voice. At the busiest corner she cries out; at the entrance of the city gates she speaks:
>
> "How long, O simple ones, will you love being simple?
>
> "How long will scoffers delight in their scoffing and fools hate knowledge?"

"Give heed to my reproof," she continues. And then she says:

> I will pour out my thoughts to you,
>   I will make my words known to you.

The first half of this verse—"I will pour out my thoughts to you"—can also be translated, "I will pour out my Spirit upon you,"[5] a function attributed to Yahweh in prophetic texts.[6] This is the first hint of a possibility that will soon become explicit: that Sophia is a personification of God.

As the passage concludes, Sophia speaks of being ignored and warns of the consequences:

> Because I have called you and you refused, have stretched out my hand and no one heeded, and because you have ignored my counsel and would have none of my reproof, I also will laugh at your calamity; I will mock when panic strikes you, when panic strikes you like a storm.[7]

Thus in this passage as a whole, Sophia's role is essentially prophetic. Though a wisdom figure, she speaks very much like the classical prophets of ancient Israel: in the marketplaces and public squares, she calls to people to heed her words and warns of calamity and disaster to befall those who ignore her counsel.

Her various roles are more fully described in an extended speech found in Proverbs 8.1–9.6. In the first half of the speech, she speaks of herself as the source of truth, insight, and strength. Indeed, "by me kings reign and rulers decree what is just." She loves those who love her, and those who seek her will find her.[8]

In the second half of the speech, she speaks of her role in creation. She was in the beginning with God before the world was created:

> Yahweh created me [Sophia] at the beginning of God's work, the first of God's acts of long ago. Ages ago I was set up, at the first, before the beginning of the earth.

Not only was Sophia with God from before the beginning, but she participated in God's creative work:

> When God established the heavens, I was there. . . . When God marked out the foundations of the earth, I was beside God as a master worker.[9]

Here there is the suggestion that it was through Sophia that God created the world. Sophia was the chief artisan who executed the divine plan.[10] The same point is made earlier in Proverbs: "Yahweh by *wisdom* founded the earth; by understanding God established the heavens."[11]

To return to chapter 8 of Proverbs, Sophia then speaks of her dwelling place in the presence of God: "I was daily God's delight, rejoicing before God." Yet she also dwells in the world; Sophia speaks of "rejoicing in the inhabited world and delighting in the human race."[12] She continues by speaking of her present role. She is the source of life: "Happy are those who keep my ways . . . ; happy is the one who listens to me . . . ; for whoever finds me finds life and obtains favor from Yahweh."[13] Finally, she concludes by inviting people to her banquet of bread and wine:

> Sophia has set her table. She has sent out her servant girls, she calls from the highest places in the town, "You that are simple, turn in here!" To those without sense, she says, "Come, eat of my bread and drink of the wine I have mixed."[14]

The Jewish personification of wisdom as Sophia, and the attribution to her of divine qualities, becomes even more developed in two intertestamental books—Sirach, and the Wisdom of Solomon.[15] In Sirach, written around 180 B.C., Sophia again speaks of her origin in God "in the beginning":

> From eternity, in the beginning, God created me, and for eternity I shall not cease to be.

She speaks of her presence everywhere:

> I came forth from the mouth of the Most High, and covered the earth like a mist. I dwelt in the highest heavens, and my throne was in a pillar of cloud. Alone I compassed the vault of heaven and traversed the depths of the abyss. Over waves of the sea, over all the earth, and over every people and nation I have held sway.

Then the author speaks of Sophia pitching her tent and dwelling in Israel. God "chose the place for her tent" among the people of Jacob, and she was in the tabernacle in the wilderness until she came to dwell in Jerusalem. Sophia is here, among other things, identical with the Shekinah, the divine presence. Finally, as in Proverbs, Sophia also hosts a banquet.[16]

In the Wisdom of Solomon, a book written near the time of Jesus, the divine qualities of Sophia are most developed.[17] Sophia is "the fashioner of all things," and the "mother" of all good things.[18] Then, in a remarkable passage, she is spoken of as:

> . . . a spirit that is intelligent, holy, unique, manifold, subtle, mobile, clear, unpolluted, distinct, invulnerable, loving the good, keen, irresistible, beneficent, humane, steadfast, sure, free from anxiety, all-powerful, overseeing all, and penetrating through all spirits. . . .

Those are, of course, all attributes of God. Moreover, like God, she is everywhere present: "she pervades and penetrates all things." Sophia "is a breath of the power of God and a pure emanation of the glory of the Almighty" and "a reflection of eternal light." Like God, she is omnipotent and the sustaining source of life:

> Although she is but one, she can do all things, and while remaining in herself, she renews all things.

She enters into relationship with people: "In every generation, she passes into holy souls." She is the source of prophetic inspiration, making people "friends of God and prophets."[19]

Finally, it is she who was active in the history of Israel from the very beginning of the Old Testament story. We are accustomed to hearing God spoken of as the one who led Israel out of Egypt. But in Wisdom of Solomon, it is Sophia who does this.

> A holy people and blameless race Sophia delivered from a nation of oppressors. . . . She brought them over the Red Sea, and led them through deep waters; she drowned their enemies, and cast them up from the depth of the sea.[20]

Thus in the book as a whole, she has qualities and functions normally attributed to God.[21]

What are we to make of the remarkable role of Sophia in the wisdom tradition of Israel? Though long noticed by scholars, it was most often seen simply as an interesting use of the literary device of personification. But more is involved, as recent scholarship has shown. In these books Sophia is closely associated with God, at times becoming indistinguishable from God in terms of the functions and qualities ascribed to her, so that one may speak of a "functional equivalency" between Sophia and God.[22] Thus the language about *Sophia* is not simply personification of wisdom in female form, but personification of *God* in female form. Sophia is a female image for God, a lens through which divine reality is imaged as a woman.[23] In short, the use of Sophia language involves female imagery for speaking of God in the biblical tradition itself.

THE SYNOPTIC GOSPELS

To turn now to the New Testament, there are a number of passages in the synoptic gospels that associate Jesus with the figure of Sophia. On one occasion, Jesus is reported to have said:

> Therefore also the Sophia of God said, "I will send them prophets and emissaries, some of whom they will kill and persecute," so that this generation may be charged with the blood of all the prophets shed since the foundation of the world.[24]

Of most importance for our purposes is the introductory phrase, in which Jesus speaks for divine Sophia. Speaking her words, he is the envoy or emissary of Sophia.

In another verse, Jesus speaks of himself as a child of Sophia. At the end of a passage that reports criticisms directed against Jesus and John the Baptizer, Jesus says:

> John the Baptizer has come eating no bread and drinking no wine; and you say, "He has a demon." The Son of man [a reference to Jesus himself] has come eating and drinking; and you say, "Behold, a glutton and a wino, a friend of tax collectors and sinners [outcasts]!" *Yet Sophia is vindicated by her children.*[25]

Here Jesus speaks of himself (and, implicitly, of the Baptizer as well) as a child of Sophia. Taken together, these two passages imply that the early Christian movement saw Jesus as both the spokesperson and the child of Sophia, and that Jesus himself may have spoken of himself in these terms.[26]

There are further associations between Sophia and the mission and message of Jesus in the synoptics. The connection to Jesus' image of God as compassionate, as "like a womb," is striking.[27] To say that God is like a womb is to say that God is like a woman, just as the personification of God as Sophia suggests that God is like a woman; and Jesus is a spokesperson for the compassion of Sophia/God. The centrality of banquets and banquet imagery, especially Jesus' festive meals with outcasts, may also be connected to Sophia. Most often scholars have connected this practice to images of the messianic age as involving a banquet with the Messiah. This is possible. However, the association of Sophia with a banquet is at least equally strong in the Jewish tradition. Perhaps the banquets of Jesus are the banquets of Sophia.

There may also be a connection to the Kingdom of God. As already noted, throughout much of this century scholars have typically understood language about the Kingdom of God to refer to the eschatological or apocalyptic Kingdom, that future coming Kingdom that was to bring an end to the world as we know it.[28] But John Dominic Crossan in his recent book on Jesus argues that, with the collapse of the apocalyptic understanding of the Kingdom, we should probably see the meaning of Jesus' Kingdom language in the context of the wisdom tradition.[29] That tradition also spoke of a Kingdom, and the Kingdom of which Jesus spoke may well be the Kingdom of Wisdom and not a Kingdom coming with the fires of the final judgment.

Some of this discussion is speculative, and whether it can be affirmed with confidence depends upon future research. But what can be said with confidence is that the synoptics portray Jesus not only as a wisdom teacher but also as one intimately related to Sophia.

PAUL

Wisdom is also a central category for the apostle Paul. As we shall see, he speaks of Jesus as the Sophia of God. But before treating that, it is illuminating to explore another connection between Paul's use of wisdom language and the alternative wisdom of Jesus.

Next to Jesus, Paul is the most important person in the history of early Christianity.[30] The genuine letters of Paul, all written in the fifteen years before his execution in Rome around the year 64, are our earliest witness to the early Christian movement. They are, of course, quite different from the gospels. For the most part written to Christian communities that Paul himself had founded, they typically address specific local problems. Paul consequently makes very little reference to the pre-Easter Jesus and his teaching, though the post-Easter Jesus—the risen living Christ—is absolutely central to his experience and theology.[31]

Yet beneath these differences between the gospels and Paul's letters, and in spite of Paul's relative silence about the historical Jesus, there is a striking similarity between the message of Paul and the subversive and alternative wisdom of Jesus. We see this most clearly in Paul's use of the language of *justification*. Considered by many to be the center of Paul's theology, it is, at the very least, one of the two or three most important notions for understanding Paul's message.

Justification is a legal metaphor. Its linguistic home in the ancient world was in a court of law, where "justified" was a verdict. Though not the exact equivalent of the modern "innocent" or "acquitted," it was the verdict one would want to hear: it meant that one had been found to be in the right. Transferred to the theological realm, justification concerned how one was made right with God.

For Paul, the heart of the gospel is that we are made right with God *by grace*. His full formula is "justification by grace through faith."[32] The opposite of justification by grace is, of course, justification by works. This is the same as "life under the law," in which one seeks to become right with God by "works of the law"—that is, by meeting God's requirements. It is, to use language introduced in chapter 4, life according to "the performance principle," in which my "okayness," whether in a religious or secular framework, depends upon something I do or believe. This is the way of being that Paul attacks with such passion in his letters.

Importantly, for Paul "life under the law" is not simply to be equated with "life under the Torah." That is, the problem was not with the Torah as such, but with a way of being that sought to be "okay" before God through the fulfillment of requirements, be they many or few. Christians sometimes misunderstand this, thinking that the problem was that the Torah had the wrong requirements, and then substituting Christian requirements instead. When this happens, "life under the law" remains.

Justification by grace, on the other hand, is justification freely given by God as a gift. Its effect is to deliver us from the life of anxious striving and of the self-preoccupation that goes with it. For Paul, this is the central significance of the gospel of Christ:

> We are now justified by God's grace as a gift through the redemption that is in Christ Jesus.
>
> Christ is the end of the law.
>
> For freedom Christ has set us free. Stand firm, therefore, and do not submit again to a yoke of slavery.[33]

Thus for Paul there are two radically different ways of being: living by grace through faith, and living under the law by works.[34] This fundamental contrast, which has been so important to Protestant theology and has often been misunderstood,[35] is the same as the contrast we find in the teaching of Jesus. "Justification by works," or "life under the law," is life in the world of conventional wisdom, with its emphasis upon requirements and rewards. Life by grace is the alternative wisdom of Jesus, with its emphasis upon the compassion and Spirit of God.

Paul explicitly used wisdom language to describe these two different ways of being in the first four chapters of 1 Corinthians, a letter written around the year 54. In response to factionalism within the Christian community in Corinth, Paul developed a strong contrast between "the wisdom of this world" and "the wisdom of God." Implicitly, the factionalists (who, it is to be remembered, were Christians) were living by "the wisdom of this world." This apparently consisted of identifying with a particular interpretation of the gospel, or possibly of identifying with a particular Christian leader. The factionalists had been saying, " 'I belong to Paul,' or 'I belong to Apollos,' or 'I belong to

Cephas.'"[36] Paul countered by speaking of "the wisdom of God" (which he also spoke of as "the foolishness of God" because it is the opposite of "the wisdom of this world"), which "destroys the wisdom of the wise." The wisdom of God is "Christ crucified," which shatters the wisdom of this world. It is grounded in "the Spirit that is from God" and not in "the spirit of the world."[37] Its fruit is unity and not division.

In short, the contrast between "the wisdom of this world" and "the wisdom of God" is the same as the contrast between conventional wisdom and the alternative wisdom of Jesus. Like Jesus, Paul subverted the world of conventional wisdom; and he spoke of an alternative wisdom grounded in the grace of God as known in Jesus. There is thus a striking continuity between the wisdom teaching of Jesus and the center of Paul's message.

In addition to this continuity, Paul also spoke explicitly of Christ as "the wisdom of God."

> We proclaim Christ crucified, a stumbling block to Jews and foolishness to Gentiles, but to those who are called, both Jews and Gentiles, Christ the power of God and *the wisdom of God*.[38]

Some lines later Paul wrote: "God is the source of your life in Christ Jesus, who became for us *wisdom from God*."[39]

In what sense is Christ the wisdom of (and from) God? In particular, are we to understand "wisdom of God" in these verses as resonating with the nuances of divine Sophia? It is possible, and if so, it means that Paul spoke of Jesus as the Sophia of and from God.[40]

There is yet one further connection between Jewish language about Sophia and the language Paul used to speak about Jesus. In a couple of passages, Paul speaks of what we call the preexistence of Christ—that is, Christ existing from eternity with God and being active in creation. The first of these is in a compact formula in 1 Corinthians:

> There is one God, the Father, from whom are all things and for
>   whom we exist;
> and one Lord, Jesus Christ, *through whom are all things and through
>   whom we exist*.[41]

The second passage, which is Pauline even if we cannot be certain that it is from Paul himself, expands the description of Christ's role in creation:

> Christ is the image of the invisible God, the firstborn of all creation; for in [or *by*] him all things in heaven and on earth were created, things visible and invisible, whether thrones or dominions or rulers or powers—all things have been created through him and for him. He himself is before all things, and in him all things hold together.[42]

The language here used about Christ is, of course, language used about Sophia in the Jewish tradition, which had shaped Paul. It not only describes Jesus in the language of divine wisdom, but in effect identifies Jesus with wisdom.[43] The preexistence of Christ is thus in fact the preexistence of divine Sophia. For Paul, Jesus is the embodiment of Sophia.

THE GOSPEL OF JOHN

The presentation of Jesus in wisdom language is even more striking in the final voice from the New Testament that we shall consider, the gospel of John. The prologue to John's gospel (which may have had its origin as an early Christian hymn, which the author of John then incorporated into the beginning of the gospel) begins with some of the best-known words in the Bible.[44] As I quote it, I will substitute the Greek word *logos* where the English translation reads "Word."

> In the beginning was the *logos*, and the *logos* was with God, and the *logos* was God. He [the *logos*] was in the beginning with God. All things came into being through him. And without him not one thing came into being that has come into being. In him was life, and the life was the light of all people. . . . He [the *logos*] was in the world, and the world came into being through him; yet the world did not know him. . . . And the *logos* became flesh and dwelt among us.[45]

It is important in these opening verses of the gospel not to think of "Word" or *logos* as referring to Jesus, if by Jesus we mean "Jesus of Nazareth." Reading it as "Jesus" is unconsciously encouraged both by the later Christian doctrine of the Trinity and by the use of masculine pronouns in the Greek original and in English translations. But masculine pronouns are used because *logos* is a masculine noun in Greek, not because the referent of *he* is Jesus. John is not saying, "In the beginning was *Jesus*," as if John thought Jesus of Nazareth was present at creation. Rather, that which became incarnate in Jesus—namely, the *logos*—was present at creation. It is the *logos* (not Jesus) that was with God and that was God.[46]

Scholars have long noted the close relationship between what John says about the *logos* and what is said about Sophia in the Jewish tradition. Sophia was present with God from the beginning, active in creation, and is present in the created world.[47] This functional equivalency between *logos* and Sophia suggests that it is legitimate to substitute Sophia for *logos*, "Wisdom" for "Word," in the prologue to John's gospel. Moreover, because Sophia is a feminine noun in Greek, the pronouns also become feminine:[48]

> In the beginning was *Sophia*, and *Sophia* was with God, and *Sophia* was God. She was in the beginning with God. All things came into being through her. And without her not one thing came into being that has come into being. In her was life, and the life was the light of all people. . . . She was in the world, and the world came into being through her, yet the world did not know her.

And then the climax is reached: "And *Sophia* became flesh and dwelt among us."[49] Jesus is the incarnation of divine Sophia, Sophia become flesh.[50]

A COMPLEMENTARITY OF CHRISTOLOGICAL IMAGES

Our exploration of the role of Sophia as wisdom in the Jewish tradition and in the New Testament discloses a number of things. It enables us to see a nice symmetry between Jesus as a teacher of wisdom and the early movement's image of him as one intimately related to Sophia. As the voice of an alternative wisdom, Jesus is also the voice of Sophia.

It also enables us to glimpse what may be the earliest Christology of the Christian movement.[51] The use of Sophia language to speak about Jesus goes back to the earliest layers of the developing tradition. It is also, as we have seen, widespread across the tradition. According to the synoptics, Paul, and John, that which was present in Jesus was the Sophia of God.

This points not only to the centrality of Sophia language in the formation of the early Christian movement, but also to a gender complementarity of Christologies. For early Christianity, Jesus was the Son of the Father and the incarnation of Sophia, the child of the intimate *Abba*, and the child of Sophia. This awareness is very helpful for us in an age of growing sensitivity to the issue of inclusive language.

It also points to the impossibility of literalizing Christological language. The multiplicity of images for speaking of Jesus' relationship to God (as *logos*, *Sophia*, Son—to name but a few) should make it clear that none of them is to be taken literally. They are metaphorical.

This is important to understand in a tradition whose Christological and devotional language has been dominated by patriarchal imagery. Trinitarian language and liturgical formulae that speak of "Father and Son" easily create the impression that this is the definitive Christian way of speaking about God and Jesus. But it is useful to realize that the dominance of father/son imagery reflects the fact that Trinitarian thinking took shape in a patriarchal and androcentric culture. To imagine the impossible: had the Trinity been formulated in a matriarchal culture, Jesus might still be spoken of as "son," but one may be quite sure that he would not be spoken of primarily as Son of *the Father*.[52]

Thus it is not the case that Jesus is *literally* "the Son of God," though he can also be spoken of metaphorically in other ways, such as the Sophia of God. Rather, both are metaphors. What they have in common is that they point to Jesus as one whose relationship to God was so intimate and deep that he could be spoken of as the son of *Abba* and the child of Sophia. We do not (and probably cannot) know whether this way of speaking began while Jesus was still alive, or whether these images were present in his own consciousness. True, it is plausible to see a connection between this language and what we can surmise about his experience. The intimacy of the metaphors is consistent with seeing the pre-Easter Jesus as a spirit person. As one who knew the Spirit, Jesus *may* have imaged and/or experienced the Spirit as *Abba* and as Sophia. But did he, in addition, think of himself as "son" (in some special sense) of the one he called *Abba?* Did he think of himself as a child or emissary of divine Sophia? Given the nature of our sources, I find it difficult to imagine how a judgment of historical probability could be reached on this particular matter.[53]

Yet though we cannot know whether these images were part of the self-understanding of Jesus, it is clear that imaging Jesus as "Son of God" and as "the wisdom of God" is in the oldest stratum of the movement's developing traditions. Thus, whether or not these images tell us anything about the consciousness of Jesus, they put us in touch with the earliest stage of the community's process of Christological image making and reflection. Strikingly, "Son of God" and "Sophia of God" are both found in that earliest stage.

The presence of both *son* and *wisdom* Christologies in the early movement affects the popular image of Jesus, the Jesus we have met before. Their presence points to gender complementarity in thinking about Jesus, which is quite new to many people. Beyond that, they also move Christological thinking out of the literalistic framework that most often accompanies the popular image. The multiplicity of early Christological images—"son" and "wisdom" and others—leads to the recognition that this language is metaphorical.

This recognition subverts the common impression that Christian faith involves believing that Jesus was *literally* "the Son of God." It is a helpful subversion. The literalistic reading of "Son of God" narrows the scope of Christology by giving primacy to one image. It also is very hard to believe, in part because of uncertainty about what is being affirmed when one says Jesus was literally the Son of God.

But when "Son of God" is seen instead as one metaphor among several, it opens up the possibility of a much richer understanding of the significance of Jesus as experienced and expressed in the early Christian movement. The issue is no longer believing that Jesus was literally the Son of God, but appreciating the richness of meaning suggested by the multiplicity of Christological images. He was "the Son," yes, but also the incarnation of the Word, which was also the Wisdom of God. He was the Son of God, the *logos* of God, and the *Sophia* of God.[54]

NOTES

1. The council at Nicea, convened soon after the emperor Constantine had converted to Christianity and declared it a legal religion, was the first ecumenical (worldwide) council of bishops. At Chalcedon (the fourth ecumenical council), the primary subject was "the two natures of Christ" (human and divine) and how they are related to each other "in one person." As a result of Nicea and Chalcedon, the questions of Christology have most often been cast in the language of "substance," "person," and "two natures." But seeing Christological questions in these categories reflects developments considerably later than the New Testament period. These developments are not "wrong"; they represent the best efforts of the church to conceptualize its doctrinal teachings in the thought categories of the time. But they tend to obscure the metaphorical and diverse Christological images of the New Testament. As I shall argue in this chapter, awareness of this diversity enriches our understanding of early Christian experience and expression.

2. George Gallup, Jr., and Jim Castelli, in *The People's Religion* (New York: Macmillan, 1989), p. 63, report that 84 percent of Americans believe that Jesus was God or the Son of God. I quite frankly do not know what to make of this statistic, and find it hard to believe. Minimally, however, it means that 84 percent think of Jesus as "God or the Son of God." *That* is the phrase they associate with him.

3. Without seeking to be comprehensive, I mention for purposes of illustration some other Christological metaphors: Jesus as "second Adam" (Paul); Jesus as "Lamb of God" (John, Revelation); Jesus as "the great high priest and sacrifice" (Hebrews); Jesus as *logos*—that is, "Word" (John). For an excellent, easily accessible article on this topic, see James D. G. Dunn, "Christology (NT)," in *The Anchor Bible Dictionary*, ed. David Noel Freedman (New York: Doubleday, 1992), vol. 1, pp. 979–91.

4. For compact, accessible treatments of Sophia in the Jewish tradition, see especially Kathleen M. O'Connor, *The Wisdom Literature* (Wilmington, DE: Michael Glazier, 1988), pp. 59–85; Elizabeth A. Johnson,

She Who Is: The Mystery of God in Feminist Discourse (New York: Crossroad, 1992), pp. 86–93; and Roland E. Murphy, "Wisdom in the Old Testament," in *The Anchor Bible Dictionary,* ed. David Noel Freedman (New York: Doubleday, 1992), vol. 6, pp. 920–31 (especially pp. 926–27). Murphy points out that the "personification of wisdom is simply unique in the Bible, both for its quantity and quality" (p. 926). See also Susan Cady, Marian Ronan, and Hal Taussig, *Sophia: The Future of Feminist Spirituality* (San Francisco: Harper & Row, 1986).

5. Proverbs 1.23; O'Connor, *The Wisdom Literature,* pp. 71–72.

6. One such text is to be found in Joel 2.28: "I [Yahweh] will pour out my spirit on all flesh."

7. Quoted verses are Proverbs 1.20–26; the whole passage is 1.20–33.

8. Proverbs 8.1–21; the verses echoed or quoted are 8.14–15, 17.

9. Quoted verses are Proverbs 8.22–23, 27a, 29b–30. "Master worker" (Proverbs 8.30) can also be translated as "nursling" or "child," but the close connection to being "beside God" in the creative acts referred to in 8.27–29 suggests that "master worker"—one assisting in creation—fits the context better.

10. So also O'Connor, *The Wisdom Literature,* p. 67.

11. Proverbs 3.19.

12. Proverbs 8.30b–31.

13. Proverbs 8.32b, 34a, 35. See also 3.13–18, where Sophia is spoken of as more precious than gold, silver, and jewels, and as "a tree of life to those who lay hold of her."

14. The banquet is described in Proverbs 9.1–6; quoted words are from 9.2b–5. Other references to the Wisdom Woman in Proverbs include 3.13–18, 4.5–9, and probably 31.10–31, a passage that has typically been seen as a description of "the ideal wife." O'Connor, in *The Wisdom Literature,* pp. 77–79, persuasively argues that the passage is best understood as a description of Sophia, for the functions of the "strong woman" are not those of any actual or potential wife in ancient Israel, given the role of women in that culture.

15. Sirach is known by a number of different names: "The Wisdom of Ben Sira," "Ecclesiasticus" (not to be confused with Ecclesiastes), and "The Wisdom of Jesus ben [son of] Sirach." It is typically abbreviated "Sir." or "Ecclus." Though Protestants put both Sirach and Wisdom of Solomon in the Apocrypha, they are canonical in the Roman Catholic and Orthodox traditions.

16. All of this is found in chap. 24 of Sirach. Quoted words are from verses 9, 3–6, 8. The banquet is referred to in 24.19–21.

17. Like the wisdom books of Proverbs and Ecclesiastes, this book is attributed to Solomon, the "patron saint" of wisdom in Israel. It is a late work, however, written by a Jewish author living in Alexandria in Egypt, probably in the first century B.C., though some suggest a first century A.D. date.

18. Wisdom of Solomon 7.22, 11–12. And, as in Proverbs and Sirach, Sophia is present from the beginning: Wisdom of Solomon 6.22.

19. This speech about Sophia, put into the mouth of Solomon, begins in Wisdom of Solomon 7.7. Quoted verses are 7.22–23, 24b–25a, 26a, 27. See also 8.6, which refers to her as "fashioner of what exists."

20. Wisdom of Solomon 10.15, 18–19. This chapter begins the story of Sophia's involvement in Israel's history with Adam and continues through Noah and the patriarchs to the exodus. The story continues into chap. 11.

21. This remarkable book has been more important in the history of Christianity than the noncanonical status given to it by Protestants would suggest. Augustine, for example, refers to it almost eight hundred times; see David Winston, "Solomon, Wisdom of" in *The Anchor Bible Dictionary,* ed. David Noel Freedman (New York: Doubleday, 1992), vol. 6, p. 127.

22. See also Johnson, *She Who Is,* p. 91; Johnson speaks of "the functional equivalence between the deeds of *Sophia* and those of the biblical God." See also her helpful review of five different understandings of Sophia language on pp. 90–93.

23. This is a recent emphasis of scholarship. See Johnson, *She Who Is,* pp. 91–92: Sophia is "Israel's God in female imagery" and "a female personification of God's own being in creative and saving involvement with the world"; "*Sophia* personified divine reality." Elisabeth Schüssler Fiorenza, in *In Memory of Her* (New York: Crossroad, 1985), p. 132, speaks of "the female *Gestalt* of divine *Sophia,*" and of God imaged "in a woman's *Gestalt* as divine *Sophia.*" According to James Dunn (cited in Johnson, *She Who Is,* p. 91 and p. 289, n. 29), Sophia is God, revealing and known. Roland Murphy, in *The Anchor Bible Dictionary,* vol. 6, p. 927, points out that Sophia is of God, born of God, in God, and then asks rhetorically, "Is Wisdom not the Lord, who turns toward creatures and summons them through creation?" O'Connor, in *The Wisdom Literature,* says: "She is herself

God" (p. 83), and "To follow Wisdom, to embrace her and to live with her, is finally to live with God" (p. 85).

24. Luke 11.49–50 = Matthew 23.34–35. It is thus a Q passage, though only Luke has the introductory phrase that refers to Sophia. It is difficult to know whether Matthew deleted it from Q or Luke added it. In favor of the former possibility is the fact that another Q passage (to be treated next) has Jesus referring to Sophia: Luke 7.35 = Matthew 11.19.

25. Luke 7.33–35 = Matthew 11.18–19. Matthew has "wisdom is vindicated by her *deeds*," whereas Luke has "by her *children*." Luke's version is more likely that of Q. See Joseph A. Fitzmyer, *The Gospel According to Luke I–IX* (New York: Doubleday, 1981), pp. 679, 681. Fitzmyer further notes that Luke probably added the word *all* to the Q saying, which originally referred to John and Jesus together as wisdom's "children." Matthew's revision actually takes the relationship between Jesus and Sophia one step further: he speaks of Jesus' deeds as the deeds of Sophia, thereby identifying Jesus with Wisdom herself. See also Matthew 11.28–30: "Come to me, all you who are weary and are carrying heavy burdens, and I will give you rest. Take my yoke upon you. . . . For my yoke is easy, and my burden is light." The passage echoes Sirach 51.23–26, which speaks of Sophia's "yoke," and therefore the Jesus of Matthew speaks *as wisdom*. On Jesus as wisdom in Matthew, see James D. G. Dunn, *The Partings of the Ways* (Philadelphia: Trinity Press International, 1991), pp. 213–15; Johnson, *She Who Is*, pp. 95–96; and sources cited by both.

26. See Schüssler Fiorenza, *In Memory of Her*, pp. 130–40 (especially pp. 132–35). On the historical Jesus and Sophia, see also Johnson, *She Who Is*, pp. 156–58.

27. See chapter 3 of this book.

28. See chapter 2 of this book, p. 29, and n. 21.

29. John Dominic Crossan, *The Historical Jesus: The Life of a Mediterranean Jewish Peasant* (San Francisco: HarperSanFrancisco, 1991), pp. 287–92.

30. Paul has a bad reputation in some contemporary Christian circles. Colleagues (including some who are teaching in seminaries) tell me that whereas most students are favorably disposed toward Jesus, many begin their study of Paul with a decidedly negative attitude. A number of factors feed this attitude. Paul is perceived as concerned with abstract and complex doctrinal matters rather than with the "simple teaching" of Jesus. He is seen as antisex, antiwomen, and

antigay. Or persons are put off by the way they have heard Paul used in Christian preaching and teaching. All of this is understandable, though most of it is unfair to Paul. The most offensive passages are in letters that he did not write, even though they have been attributed to him (see chap. 3, n. 43). Moreover, as I shall argue, beneath the differences between Paul and Jesus there is a striking similarity.

31. It is difficult to know what to make of Paul's relative silence about the teaching of Jesus. Is he silent—as some have argued, especially during that part of this century when the quest for the historical Jesus was in eclipse—because only the risen Christ (and not the pre-Easter Jesus) mattered to Paul? Or is the silence simply a result of the nature of Paul's writings—namely, letters to communities that he had founded? Perhaps Paul had already communicated in person what was most important about the pre-Easter Jesus.

32. Justification by grace is an especially important topic for Paul in Galatians and Romans.

33. Romans 3.24; Romans 10.4.; Galatians 5.1.

34. The stark contrast between justification by grace and justification by works is closely related to a number of contrasts in Paul's writings. As a dialectical thinker, Paul thought in opposites: grace versus law, faith versus works, life "in Christ" versus life "in Adam," the "fruits of the Spirit" versus the "works of the flesh," freedom versus slavery. All of these contrasts are ways of speaking of two radically different ways of being.

35. See chapter 4, pp. 79–80, where I note how in Christian circles "faith" often comes to be understood as the new requirement replacing the requirement of "works." However, in order to be true to Paul's understanding of "justification by grace through faith," faith cannot be understood as a requirement (which would make it a "work"). How then can it be understood? It is helpful to think of faith as "the *realization* of grace," in two senses of that word. *To realize* can mean "to come to see," as when we say, "Now I realize what you mean." Faith as the realization of grace thus means "coming to see that God/reality is gracious." If one does not see that, one remains in the world of requirements, performance, and anxious striving. Less commonly, *to realize* can mean "to make real," or "to actualize." I think faith has this meaning, too: to actualize or make real the new way of being, the life under grace.

36. 1 Corinthians 1.12.

37. Respectively, 1 Corinthians 1.19, 23; 2.12.

38. 1 Corinthians 1.23–24. It is interesting to speculate about why "Christ crucified" is a stumbling block to Jews. The notion of a crucified Messiah was apparently unknown in the Jewish tradition, and was perhaps an impossible combination of terms. It may function as a koan does in Zen Buddhism—namely, as a paradox that shatters accepted ways of thinking. It thus may be a "Christian koan."

39. 1 Corinthians 1.30.

40. Schüssler Fiorenza, *In Memory of Her*, pp. 188–92; she includes these verses in her data base for arguing that the pre-Pauline (and thus very early) Christian missionary movement had a "*Sophia* christology." She also cites the following pre-Pauline hymns or hymn fragments as reflecting Sophia theology: Philippians 2.6–11; 1 Timothy 3.16; Colossians 1.15–20; Ephesians 2.14–16; Hebrews 1.3; 1 Peter 3.18, 22; John 1.1–14.

41. 1 Corinthians 8.6.

42. Colossians 1.15–17. Colossians (along with Ephesians and 2 Thessalonians) is among those letters about which scholars are divided regarding whether they were written by Paul himself. To say that Colossians is Pauline indicates that it has strong affinities with Paul's thought, whether written by him or not. For a compact treatment of the question, see Victor P. Furnish, "Colossians," in *The Anchor Bible Dictionary*, ed. David Noel Freedman (New York: Doubleday, 1992), vol 1, pp. 1090–96.

43. See especially Dunn, *Partings of the Ways*, pp. 195–97.

44. John 1.1–18. If this passage is based on an early Christian hymn, verses 6–8 (which speak of John the Baptizer) appear to be an insertion added by the author of the gospel.

45. John 1.1–4, 10, 14.

46. "Jesus" is first referred to in verse 14: "The *logos* became flesh and dwelt among us." These few words are, in effect, John's story of Jesus' birth. The tendency to hear the whole of the prologue as referring to Jesus is illustrated by a recent conversation following a lecture in which I had said that the historical Jesus was not omniscient—that as a first-century person Jesus probably thought that the earth was at the center of the universe, that it was flat, and so forth. My questioner, an intelligent, well-educated Christian lawyer, said that he thought Jesus would have known that the earth was round, the sun at the center of the solar system, and so forth because Jesus had

been present at creation and would have *seen* it all. His basis for thinking so was his reading the whole of John 1 as if it referred to Jesus of Nazareth.

47. One more similarity may be cited. Verse 10 of John's prologue says that even though the *logos* was in the world, "yet the world did not know the *logos.*" So also with Wisdom/*Sophia*: in the Jewish tradition, it is often said that she was ignored.

48. See Stevan Davies, *The New Testament: A Contemporary Introduction* (San Francisco: Harper & Row, 1988), p. 169. The claim that "Wisdom" (as much as or more than *logos*) lies behind the Johannine prologue is quite old; see Samuel Terrien, *The Elusive Presence* (San Francisco: Harper & Row, 1978), p. 418, and sources cited there. Davies suggests that the author of John uses the masculine noun *logos* rather than the feminine noun *sophia* because Jesus was male. For further comments about why John may have chosen *logos* rather than *sophia*, see Johnson, *She Who Is*, pp. 97–98.

49. There is a further connection. The Greek word translated "dwelt" actually means "tabernacled" or "tented." This is said about Sophia in Sirach 24: she "tented" within Israel. The importance of wisdom categories is not restricted to John's prologue, but runs throughout the gospel. See Dunn, *Partings of the Ways*, pp. 226–27, and sources cited there.

50. Even Saint Augustine, not typically thought of as having much feminist sensitivity, speaks of Jesus as the incarnation of Sophia: "She was sent in one way that she might be with human beings; and she has been sent another way that *she herself might be a human being.*" *De Trin* 4.20.27; cited in Johnson, *She Who Is*, pp. 156–57.

51. See also Schüssler Fiorenza, *In Memory of Her*, p. 134; and Dunn, *Partings of the Ways*, p. 195: wisdom is "probably the single most important category in the development of earliest christology."

52. See Sandra M. Schneiders's interview on the multiplicity and metaphoricity of images for God in the Bible: "God Is More than Two Men and a Bird," *U.S. Catholic*, May 1990, pp. 20–27. I find her title especially illuminating.

53. To every attempt to speak of "the christology of Jesus" (if by that one means whether he held ideas about himself similar in some ways to the post-Easter estimate of him), one can only say, "It could be so, but it could so easily be the product of the community." Perhaps more than any other part of the developing tradition, "christological" passages must be systematically suspect: they represent the

area of the community's imaging and thinking that underwent the greatest development after Easter. This judgment, I want to emphasize, applies to the question of Christology in particular, and not to the gospel tradition in its entirety (I think we can make quite strong historical probability arguments about many parts of the tradition).

54. To illustrate the claim that all Christological language is metaphorical, I share a story that I owe to John Dominic Crossan. Asked by an exasperated questioner, "Do you believe Jesus was the Son of God or don't you?" Crossan replied, "Yes—I believe he was the Son of God, and the Word of God, and the Lamb of God." The point of the reply is clear, even though it was not appreciated by the questioner (who said, "You theologians! You're all alike!"). Just as Jesus is not *literally* "the Lamb of God" (he was not a sheep), and not *literally* the Word of God (what would that mean?), so also he is not *literally* "the Son of God" (what would it mean for this to be literally true— biological sonship?). Rather, all involve the metaphorical use of images.

6

Images of Jesus and Images of the Christian Life

I began this book by underlining the important and often quite unconscious connection between images of Jesus and images of the Christian life. The close relationship between the two means that what is at stake in how we think of Jesus is, to a considerable extent, how we think of the Christian life.

The image of Jesus I have sketched in the preceding chapters is quite different from the popular image of Jesus, the Jesus many of us have met before. His own self-understanding did not include thinking and speaking of himself as the Son of God whose historical intention or purpose was to die for the sins of the world, and his message was not about believing in him. Rather, he was a spirit person, subversive sage, social prophet, and movement founder who invited his followers and hearers into a transforming relationship with the same Spirit that he himself knew, and into a community whose social vision was shaped by the core value of compassion. Naturally, this image of Jesus leads to a quite different image of the Christian life, many of whose characteristics have already been identified.

119

In this concluding chapter, I want to broaden our framework for thinking about images of Jesus and images of the Christian life to include the Bible as a whole, especially the Old Testament. There are two reasons for enlarging our framework. The first has to do with us: just as our image of Jesus shapes our image of the Christian life, so does our image of Scripture. In part, this is because we learned about Jesus in the context of the Bible, and our sense of what the Bible is about will affect our sense of what Jesus was about. Scripture shapes our understanding of Jesus. The second reason has to do with Jesus and the early Christian movement. Both he and his followers were rooted in Judaism, and the sacred traditions of Israel—the Old Testament—shaped their ways of seeing, thinking, and speaking.

In our effort to see the significance of Scripture for them and us, we shall be greatly aided by a relatively recent emphasis in biblical and theological scholarship. In the last two decades, a movement known as *story theology* has called attention to the narratival character of the Bible, or, to say the same thing, the centrality of "story" in Jewish and Christian scriptures.[1]

This can be seen in three features of the Bible. There is the narrative framework of the Bible as a whole, which on a grand scale can be considered as a single story beginning with paradise and paradise lost in the opening chapters of Genesis, moving through the story of God's redeeming activity in Israel and through Jesus, and concluding with the vision of paradise restored in the final vision of the book of Revelation. The centrality of narrative in the Bible is also pointed to by the fact that it contains literally hundreds of individual stories. And, finally, at the center of Scripture are a small number of "macro-stories"— the primary stories that shaped the religious imagination and life of ancient Israel and the early Christian movement.

Story theology not only emphasizes the centrality of story in the biblical tradition, but also criticizes much of Christian theology and modern historical scholarship for having obscured or eclipsed this feature. Theology, with its natural inclination toward conceptualization, has typically sought to extract a core of meaning from a story, which is then expressed in nonnarrative form. The story as story is lost. Modern historical study of the Bible has also tended to lose the story, either by seeking the history behind the story or by an analytical approach that often loses the story by focusing on its bits and pieces. In both cases, the story as story disappears.

Story theology seeks to recapture the story character of Scripture. Though it is a recent movement, its approach is very ancient. To a large extent, the Bible has its origins in story and storytelling. One should perhaps imagine the people of ancient Israel telling the stories of their ancestors around campfires, to the accompaniment of drums. The image is undoubtedly romantic, but it also catches a truth: much of the biblical tradition originated in and was carried by storytelling. So also with the gospels; their traditions about Jesus were transmitted as stories long before they became texts.

Moreover, the story character of Scripture applies not only to its origins. It also applies to how Scripture was experienced for most of the centuries of the Jewish and Christian traditions. Ordinary people living in preprint cultures (that is, living prior to the invention of the printing press about five hundred years ago) knew the Bible not as texts but as stories. The stories were transmitted and experienced in a variety of ways: visually, in the images of Christian art, especially in the stained-glass windows of the churches of the Middle Ages and afterward; musically, in hymns and popular ballads; verbally, in sermons; and ritually, in worship and in the great festivals and feast days of the church year.

As a particular form of religious discourse, stories function in a particular way. Religious laws speak of how to behave; theology and doctrine speak of how to understand and what to believe; but stories appeal to the imagination, to that place within us where our images of reality, life, and ourselves reside. The great stories of the Bible image what the religious life is about. In the rest of this chapter, I will describe what seem to me to be the most important stories in the biblical tradition. Understanding them and how they image the religious life can greatly enrich our imaging of Jesus and our imaging of the Christian life.

THE MACRO-STORIES OF SCRIPTURE

My central claim is that there are three "macro-stories" at the heart of Scripture that shape the Bible as a whole, and that each of these stories images the religious life in a particular way.[2] Two of the stories are grounded in the history of ancient Israel: the story of the exodus from Egypt, and the story of the exile and return from Babylon. The third, the priestly story, is grounded not in the history of ancient Israel but in an institution—namely, the temple, priesthood, and sacrifice. As the three most central stories of the Hebrew Bible, they shaped the religious imagination and understanding of both ancient Israel and the early Christian movement.[3]

As I briefly describe these stories, I will emphasize how each images what the religious life is most centrally about. The foundation for this approach is William James's simple but brilliant insight in the rich concluding chapter of his book *The Varieties of Religious Experience.* James states that the religious traditions of the world, reduced to what they have in common, make two claims. First, they claim that something is wrong with our lives as we typically live them; that is, they contain a description of the human condition or the human predicament. Second, they speak of a solution to that problem.[4]

To use a medical metaphor, the various religious traditions provide a diagnosis of the human condition and a prescription for a cure. From James's insight flow the two questions that I will address in discussing the macro-stories of Scripture: how does each of these stories image the human condition, and how does each image the solution? To put that only slightly differently, how does each image us and our lives in relation to God?

The Exodus Story

For the people of ancient Israel, the story of the exodus from Egypt was their "primal narrative." It was the most important story they knew. It was the primary story shaping their identity, their sense of who they were, and their sense of God.[5] Around it Israel's foundation document, the Pentateuch (the first five books of the Bible, also known as the Torah or Law), came into existence.

As the story that stood at the center of Israel's most ancient recital of her origins, it was to be told by parents to their children:

You shall say to your children, "We were Pharaoh's slaves in Egypt, but Yahweh brought us out of Egypt with a mighty hand. Yahweh displayed before our eyes great and awesome signs and wonders against Egypt, against Pharaoh and all his household. Yahweh brought us out from there in order to bring us in, to give us the land that Yahweh promised on oath to our ancestors."[6]

The story was remembered and celebrated liturgically again and again, preeminently in the annual festival of Passover. Importantly, it was seen not simply as a story about the past, but as a story about the present. It was not just the ancestors living in the exodus generation who were Pharaoh's slaves in Egypt and who were led out of Egypt by God. Rather, as the Passover liturgy states:

> For ever after, *in every generation, all of us must think of ourselves as having gone forth from Egypt.* For we read in the Torah: "In that day thou shalt teach thy child, saying: All this is because of what God did for me when I went forth from Egypt." *It was not only our ancestors that the Holy One, blessed be God, redeemed; us, too, the living, God redeemed together with them,* as we learn from the verse in the Torah: "And God brought us out from thence, so that God might bring us home, and give us the land which God pledged to our ancestors."[7]

Thus it is a story not only about ancient Israel, but also about "us, too, the living." As a story about both the past and the present, it images the human condition and God's relationship to us in all times.

What is this story about? Most basically, it is a story of bondage, liberation, a journey, and a destination. It begins with the Hebrews as slaves in Egypt under the lordship of Pharaoh. Life in Egypt is marked by a politics of oppression, an economics of affluence, and a religion of legitimation.[8] Though perhaps a comfortable life for members of Pharaoh's household, for those enslaved it is a life of hard labor and groaning and meager rations, with enough to survive on, but not much more. The story then moves through the plagues and the liberation itself (the word *exodus* literally means "the way out" or "the road out"). But leaving Egypt is not the end of the story. Coming out from under the lordship of Pharaoh brings the people into the wilderness and sets them upon a journey that lasts for forty years, and the destination of the journey is the promised land, which symbolically is the place of God's presence.

As a story about God and us, what is it saying? Our problem, according to this story, is that we live in Egypt, the land of bondage. We are slaves of an alien lord, the lord of Egypt, Pharaoh. It provocatively images the human condition as bondage, an image with both cultural-political and psychological-spiritual dimensions of meaning. It invites us to ask, "To what am I in bondage, and to what are we in bondage?"

The answer for most of us is "Many things." We are in bondage to cultural messages about what we should be like and what we should pursue—messages about success, attractiveness, gender roles, the good life. We are in bondage to voices from our own past, and to addictions of various kinds.

The Pharaoh who holds us in bondage is inside of us as well as outside of us. Who is the Pharaoh within me who has me enslaved and who will not let me go? What instruments of fear and oppression does he use, this Pharaoh who tries everything to remain in control? What plagues must strike him?

If the problem is bondage, the solution, of course, is liberation. In the story of the exodus itself, the liberation begins at night, in the darkness before dawn. It means leaving Egypt and the kingdom and dominion of Pharaoh. It involves passing through the sea to the other side, a passage from one kind of life to another. Liberation involves coming out from under the lordship of Pharaoh and the lordship of culture.

But liberation is not the end of the story. Rather, "the way out" leads to a journey through the wilderness. As the place beyond the domestication of culture, the wilderness is a place of freedom, where God is encountered and known. Yet it can also be a place of fear and anxiety, where we erect one golden calf after another, and where we sometimes find ourselves longing for the security of Egypt—for the "fleshpots" of Egypt, as the story puts it. At least there was food in Egypt. But the wilderness is also a place where we are nourished by God, by water from the rock and bread from heaven, and where God journeys with us in a pillar of cloud by day and a column of fire by night. The journey lasts a long time—forty years, according to the story. Its destination is life in the presence of God. Yet God is not simply the destination, but one who is known on the journey. It is a journeying *toward* God that is also *with* God.

Thus, as an epiphany of the human condition and the solution, the story of the exodus images the religious life as a journey from the life of bondage to life in the presence of God. Though we find ourselves in bondage to Pharaoh, it proclaims, there is a way out. Through signs and wonders, through the great and mighty hand of God, God can liberate us, indeed wills our liberation and yearns for our liberation, from life in bondage to culture to life as a journeying with God.

The Story of Exile and Return

Like the exodus story, the story of exile and return is grounded in a historical experience. The exile began in 587 B.C., when, after Jerusalem and its temple were conquered and destroyed by Babylon, some of the Jewish survivors were marched into exile in Babylon some eight hundred miles away. There they lived as refugees, separated from their homeland and under conditions of oppression.[9] The exile came to an end in 539 B.C., some fifty years after it began, when the Babylonian empire was conquered by the Persians, whose imperial policy allowed displaced persons to return to their homelands.

Next to the exodus, this experience of exile and return was the most important historical event shaping the life and religious imagination of the Jewish people.[10] It seared itself into their consciousness and became for them a metaphor for their relationship with God.

As an image about God and us, as an epiphany of the human condition and the solution, what is it saying? What is life in exile like? We live in a century in which millions of exiles and refugees know this experience firsthand. For the rest of us, it is fruitful to imagine what life in exile is like. It is an experience of separation from all that is familiar and dear. It usually involves powerlessness and marginality, often oppression and victimization. Like the metaphor of bondage in the exodus story, it has psychological as well as cultural-political dimensions.

As a life of being separated from that to which one belongs, exile is often marked by grief, as in one of the psalms of exile: "By the rivers of Babylon, there we sat down and wept when we remembered Zion."[11] The same sadness is expressed in one of the church's great Advent hymns: "O Come O Come Immanuel, and ransom captive Israel, that *mourns in lonely exile here.*" Israel's exile is our exile, and life in exile is marked by deep sadness and an aching loneliness.

The feeling of being separated from home and longing for home runs deeply within us. It is this yearning that gave so much power to the popular movie *E.T.* a decade ago. Those of us who saw the movie can remember the poignancy of the little green extraterrestrial pointing his finger at the sky and saying in a haunting voice filled with prolonged yearning, "Home." It is the same longing that comes to expression in the gospel hymn "Softly and tenderly Jesus is calling, calling to you and to me," with its chorus, "Come home, come home. Ye who are weary, come home."

In our own lives, the experience of exile as estrangement or alienation can be felt as a flatness, a loss of connection with a center of vitality and meaning, when one day becomes very much like another and nothing has much zest. We yearn for something that we perhaps only vaguely remember. Life in exile thus has a profound existential meaning. It is living away from Zion, the place where God is present. Indeed, exile is central in the symbolism of the Garden of Eden story in the book of Genesis. The garden—paradise—is the place of God's presence, but we live outside of the garden, east of Eden.

If our problem is exile, what is the solution? The solution is, of course, a journey of return. The invitation to return sounds throughout the second half of the book of Isaiah, spoken by a prophet whose name is not even known to us but whose words are among the most magnificent in the Hebrew Bible:

In the wilderness prepare the way of Yahweh, make straight in the desert a highway for our God.

Every valley shall be lifted up, and every mountain and hill be made low; the uneven ground shall become level, and the rough places a plain.[12]

The language images a way of return, a highway being built in the wilderness, leading from Babylon back to the promised land, back home.

Thus, like the exodus story, the story of exile and return is a journey story. It images the religious life as a journey to the place where God is present, a homecoming, a journey of return.[13] And like the exodus story, this story speaks of God aiding and assisting those who undertake the journey:

> God gives power to the faint,
> And strengthens the powerless.
> Even youths will faint and be weary,
> And the young will fall exhausted;
> But those who wait for Yahweh
> Shall renew their strength,
> They shall mount up with wings like eagles,
> They shall run and not be weary,
> They shall walk and not faint.[14]

The Priestly Story

As mentioned earlier, the third story is grounded not in a particular historical event, but in an institution of ancient Israel—namely, the temple, priesthood, and sacrifice. Within this story, the priest is the one who makes us right with God by offering sacrifice on our behalf.

The priestly story leads to a quite different image of the religious life. It is not primarily a story of bondage, exile, and journey, but a story of sin, guilt, sacrifice, and forgiveness.[15] Central to it are notions of impurity, defilement, and uncleanness, or that primal sense of "being stained" referred to by Paul Ricoeur.[16] It is therefore also linked to images of cleansing, washing, and covering over.

How does this story image the human condition? Who are we within this story? Not primarily people in bondage, or people yearning to return home. Rather, within this story, we are primarily sinners who have broken God's laws, and who therefore stand guilty before God, the lawgiver and judge. Seen through the lens of this story, the religious life becomes a story of sin, guilt, and forgiveness.

JESUS AND THE MACRO-STORIES OF SCRIPTURE

All three of these stories shape the message of Jesus, the New Testament, and subsequent Christian theology. Jesus' own message speaks of the bondage and exile caused by the world of conventional wisdom, and of the sense of sinfulness and impurity generated by the purity system. The New Testament authors speak of the meanings of Jesus' life, death, and resurrection with imagery drawn from all three stories.

These stories have also shaped the church's theology about Jesus over the centuries. In his still-classic work on the atonement, the Swedish theologian Gustaf Aulen some sixty years ago identified three main understandings of the death and resurrection of Jesus in the history of Christian theology.[17] Aulen argues that the oldest of these is one he calls *Christus Victor*, a Latin phrase that means "Christ victorious." It is an image that understands the central work of Christ to be a triumphing over "the powers" that hold humans in bondage, including sin, death, and the devil. Like the exodus story, this image sees the human predicament as bondage and the work of Christ as liberation. "The powers" holding us in bondage are Pharaoh and Egypt on a cosmic scale.

Aulen calls the second major understanding of the death and resurrection of Christ the "substitutionary" or "objective" image. This image pictures the death of Jesus as a sacrifice for sin that makes God's forgiveness possible. Though sacrificial language is used to speak of the death of Jesus in the New Testament itself, Aulen argues that this understanding of Jesus' death did not become dominant in the church until the early Middle Ages.[18] This image clearly sees the death of Jesus through the lens of the priestly story.

A third understanding of Christ's death and resurrection can, with some modification, be correlated with the exile story.[19] This third understanding portrays Jesus neither as the one who triumphs over the powers nor as a sacrifice for sin, but as "revelation" or "disclosure." The emphasis is not upon Jesus *accomplishing* something that objectively changes the relationship between God and us, but upon Jesus *revealing* something that is true.

What is revealed is more than one thing. Sometimes the emphasis is upon Jesus revealing what God is like (for example, love or compassion). Sometimes the emphasis is upon Jesus as "the light" who beckons us home from the darkness of exile. Sometimes the emphasis is upon Jesus' death and resurrection as the embodiment of the way of return, a disclosure of the internal spiritual process that brings us into an experiential relationship with the Spirit of God. Within this way of seeing Jesus, he is the incarnation of the path of return from exile.

Yet, though all three stories were important for Jesus, the early movement, and subsequent Christian theology, one of them—the priestly story—has dominated the popular understanding of Jesus and the Christian life to the present day. It is, of course, the core element in the popular image of Jesus as the dying savior whose death is a sacrifice for our sins, thereby making our forgiveness by God possible. To say "Jesus died for our sins" is to interpret his significance within the framework of the priestly story.

The centrality of the priestly story in Christian practice is illustrated not only by the popular image of Jesus but also by the prominent place given to the confession of sins in Christian worship. To speak from my own experience growing up as a Lutheran, confessing our sins was part of every Sunday-morning service:

> We poor sinners confess unto thee that we are by nature sinful and unclean, and that we have sinned against thee by thought, word, and deed. Wherefore we flee for refuge to thine infinite mercy, seeking and imploring thy grace, for the sake of our Lord Jesus Christ.

Though the words vary, similar confessions have been a regular part of Sunday worship in almost all mainline Protestant denominations. The emphasis upon confession is perhaps even greater in the Roman Catholic tradition, where the confessional was institutionalized and (until very recently) frequent personal confession was mandatory.

Thus the priestly story of sin, guilt, sacrifice, and forgiveness is most commonly the primary story shaping our sense of who we are, our image of Jesus and of what God requires, and the nature of the Christian life. Because I am about to be very critical of the priestly story, I want first to acknowledge its power and its positive meaning. The image of Jesus as a sacrifice for our sins is a sign of God's great love for us, as that familiar verse from childhood so compactly puts it: "For God so loved the world that He gave his only begotten son."[20]

The priestly story's meaning is simple, direct and radical: we are accepted, just as we are. The old gospel hymn has it right: "Just as I am, without one plea." God loves us just as we are. We are precious in God's sight. The priestly story means that our own sense of sin, impurity, and guilt need not stand between us and God. It means that new beginnings are possible; we do not need to be held in bondage by the burden of our past. And some people—those for whom the central issue in their lives is guilt or a radically negative sense of self-worth—very much need to hear this message.

But when the priestly story becomes the dominant story or the only story for imaging Jesus and the Christian life, it has serious limitations. Indeed, *limitations* is too weak a term. When it dominates Christian thinking, it produces severe distortions in our understanding of the Christian life.[21] I shall list six such distortions.

The priestly story leads to a static understanding of the Christian life, making it into a repeated cycle of sin, guilt, and forgiveness. We are absolved each Sunday, only to sin again during the week, and the cycle repeats itself. The priestly story does not often generate the question, You are accepted—now what?

Similarly, it creates a quite passive understanding of the Christian life, in at least two senses. It leads to a passivity about the religious life itself. Rather than seeing that life as a process of spiritual transformation, it stresses believing that God has already done what needs to be done. It leads to a passivity toward culture as well. One can see this by imagining how our vision of the Christian life would be different if our church services regularly included a description of the human condition flowing from the other two macro-stories, either instead of or alternating with the confession of sin. What if we were to say, "We are Pharaoh's slaves in Egypt, and we beseech you for liberation"? Or "We live in Babylon, and we ask you for deliverance"? One can understand why the church during the many centuries that it was the official religion of Western culture emphasized the confession of sin rather than saying that the culture we live in is Egypt or Babylon. The priestly story is a politically domesticating story. The stories of bondage in Egypt and exile in Babylon are culturally subversive stories.

The priestly story tends also to lead to an understanding of Christianity as primarily a religion of the afterlife. The crucial issue becomes being right with God before we die: believe now for the sake of salvation later.

The priestly story images God primarily as lawgiver and judge. God's requirements must be met, and because we cannot meet them, God graciously provides the sacrifice that meets those requirements. Yet the sacrifice generates a new requirement: God will forgive those who believe that Jesus was the sacrifice, and will not forgive those who do not believe. God's forgiveness becomes contingent or conditional. Not only is it only for those who believe, but it lasts only until sin is committed again, which can then be removed only by repentance. Thus, though the priestly story speaks of God as gracious, it places the grace of God within a system of requirements. The overarching image for God's relationship to us is a legal metaphor, which pictures God as the giver and enforcer of a set of requirements. The priestly story most often turns the subversive wisdom of Jesus into Christian conventional wisdom.

Moreover, this story is very hard to believe. The notion that God's only son came to this planet to offer his life as a sacrifice for the sins of the world, and that God could not forgive us without that having happened, and that we are saved by believing this story, is simply incredible. Taken metaphorically, this story can be very powerful. But taken literally, it is a profound obstacle to accepting the Christian message. To many people, it simply makes no sense, and I think we need to be straightforward about that.

Finally, there is one more problem with the priestly story: some people do not feel much guilt. It is difficult to know what to make of this. Perhaps some people should feel guilt who do not. But some honestly do not; guilt is not the central issue in their lives. Yet they may have strong feelings of bondage, or strong feelings of alienation and estrangement. For these people, the priestly story has nothing to say.

To maintain that it should speak to them would be like saying that Moses should have gone into Egypt and said to the Hebrew slaves, "My children, your sins are forgiven." They would properly have responded, "What? What does that have to do with us? Our problem isn't that we are sinners, you idiot. Our problem is that we are slaves, oppressed by Pharaoh!"

So it is in our own time. For some people, the central life issue is not sin and guilt, but bondage to or victimization by one Pharaoh or another. For them, what does the message of sin and forgiveness mean? Unfortunately, it often comes to mean "You should forgive the person who is victimizing you," when what the victim needs to hear is "It is not God's will that you be in bondage to that (or any) Pharaoh." Or if the central problem is alienation and meaninglessness, the message the person needs to hear is "It is not God's will that you remain in Babylon, not God's will that you mourn in lonely exile there."

Yet when the priestly story is understood as one of three ways of imaging the Christian life, rather than the primary way, the problems with it largely disappear. We can see this by identifying four elements that the macro-stories of Scripture share.

First, all of them are stories of suffering and of being at an experiential distance from God. According to the exodus story, we live a life of hard labor in Egypt, in bondage to an alien lord. According to the exile story, we live in Babylon, estranged from the center of our being and yearning. According to the priestly story, our lives are marked by guilt, shame, negative self-worth, and the experiential distance from God generated by those feelings.

Second, all of them make powerful affirmations not just about the human condition but also about God. They are stories about God, not just about us, and they portray God as intimately involved with human life. There is a power that wills our liberation, a light shining in the darkness that invites us home from exile, a compassionate presence that accepts us just as we are, though we may not yet know that.

Third, all of them are thus stories of hope. Their consistent message is that God does not will our present condition, but wills something very different for us. All of them speak about new beginnings brought about by God. The exodus story speaks of liberation from victimization and bondage, the exile story speaks the good news of "coming home," and the priestly story affirms that our own past is not the final word about us.

Fourth and finally, all are stories of a journey. This is self-evidently the case in the exodus and exile stories. Each images the religious life not as a static cycle of sin, guilt, and forgiveness, but as a journey. It is a journey leading from Egypt and Babylon into the wilderness. It is a journey of liberation and homecoming. It is a journeying toward God that is also with God. So also the priestly story, properly understood, is a journey story. In the Bible itself, the regulations governing priesthood and sacrifice (and thus the institutionalization of the priestly story) are set in the context of the journey from Egypt to the promised land.[22] In the context of a journey story, the priestly story means that God accepts us just as we are, wherever we are on our journey. Moreover, the internalization of the new identity conferred by the priestly story—that I am accepted by God, beloved by God—is a process that can take years. That process is itself a journey.

So even the priestly story is a journey story. It is when it is separated from the other journey stories of Scripture that it leads to the distortion and impoverishment of the Christian life of which I have spoken.

Thus we have three macro-stories for imaging the religious life. One might think of them as constituting a pastoral "tool kit," each addressing a different dimension of the human condition. For some, the need is liberation; for others, the need is homecoming; and for still others, the need is acceptance. But beneath their differences the stories all image the Christian life as a journey whose central quality is a deepening and transforming relationship with God.

JESUS AND THE CHRISTIAN LIFE AS JOURNEY

The story of Jesus, and our understanding of the Christian life, are much richer and fuller when we see them in the context of all three of these stories, and not simply in the context of the priestly story. All three stories informed and shaped Jesus' own perception of the religious life and therefore his message and activity.

The conventional wisdom that he subverted had characteristics of both bondage and exile, Egypt and Babylon. Conventional wisdom is life under the lordship of culture, which is both oppressive and alienating, and his message is filled with the theme of liberation and return. He came to "set the captives free," language that connects to the imagery of both bondage and exile. The story of the prodigal is shaped at a deep level by the exile story: the prodigal goes into a "far country," far from his home, and the solution to his predicament is a journey of return, a journey "home."

The emphasis both in Jesus' teaching and in the gospels themselves upon a "way" or "path" also points to an understanding of the religious life as a journey. Jesus teaches a "way," and the gospels are about "the way."[23]

Jesus' relationship to the priestly story is somewhat different. Here he subverts the story itself. His subversion of the purity system undercuts the priestly story's image of the human condition as "stained" or impure. He forgives sins apart from the institution of temple, priest, and sacrifice, thereby negating their necessity.

This subversion of the priestly story continues in Hebrews, the New Testament document that makes the greatest use of it. The central metaphor of the letter to the Hebrews portrays Jesus as the great high priest who is also the sacrifice, offering up his life as "the once for all" sacrifice for the sins of the world. The effect of this, according to Hebrews, is that the system of priesthood and sacrifice has now been abolished; in short, the author of Hebrews uses the priestly story to subvert the priestly story.[24] Strikingly, within the traditions of the early Christian movement, the priestly story was used to negate the priestly story.[25]

Thus the message of Jesus and of the New Testament as a whole is shaped by all three of the macro-stories at the center of the Hebrew Bible, albeit each of the stories functions in different ways. The priestly story is subverted, and the understanding of the religious life imaged by the journey stories affirmed. In addition, the New Testament has a journey story of its own—the story of discipleship. The meaning of the word *disciple* is the initial clue. It does not mean to be "a student of a teacher," but rather to be "a follower after somebody." Discipleship in the New Testament is, of course, a following after Jesus, a journeying with Jesus.

What picture of discipleship do we get by looking at the stories in the gospels about the relationship between Jesus and his disciples?[26] I invite you to hear what is said as resonating both with what it meant for his first followers to be in relationship to the pre-Easter Jesus and what it means to followers in every generation to be in relationship to the post-Easter Jesus. Like the macro-stories of the Old Testament, the story of discipleship is not just about the past, not just about "them," but also about us.

As a journeying with Jesus, discipleship means being on the road with him. It means to be an itinerant, a sojourner; to have nowhere to lay one's head, no permanent resting place. It means undertaking the journey from the life of conventional wisdom, from life in our Egypt and life in our Babylon, to the alternative wisdom of life in the Spirit. To journey with Jesus means listening to his teaching—sometimes understanding it, sometimes not quite getting it. It can involve denying him, even betraying him.

That journey is in his company, in his presence. There is joy in his presence. As the Dutch Roman Catholic scholar Edward Schillebeeckx comments in his quite wonderful and dense academic study of Jesus, "Being sad in Jesus' presence [was] an existential impossibility."[27] Perhaps one might feel sadness, but not sadness about existence itself.

Discipleship means eating at his table and experiencing his banquet. That banquet is an inclusive banquet, including not just me and not just us, but those we tend to exclude. It means being nourished by him and fed by him. Such seems to be the point of Jesus feeding the five thousand in the wilderness, just as Israel was fed in the wilderness on the journey in the exodus story. If we think of the eucharist as like those meals in the wilderness, it becomes a powerful symbol of journeying with Jesus and being fed by him on that journey. "Take, eat, lest the journey be too great for you."

Journeying with Jesus also means to be in a community, to become part of the alternative community of Jesus. Discipleship is not an individual path, but a journey in a company of disciples.[28] It is the road less traveled, yet discipleship involves being in a community that remembers and celebrates Jesus. Though that is not the only role of the church, it is its primary role. To use John Shea's very apt description of the church, "Gather the folks, tell the stories, break the bread."[29]

And discipleship involves becoming compassionate. "Be compassionate as God is compassionate" is the defining mark of the follower of Jesus. Compassion is the fruit of life in the Spirit and the ethos of the community of Jesus.

Thus we have what I would call a *transformist* understanding of the Christian life, an image of the Christian life richer and fuller than the fideistic and moralistic images I described in chapter 1.[30] It is a vision of the Christian life as a journey of transformation, exemplified by the story of discipleship as well as by the exodus and exile stories. It leads from life under the lordship of culture to the life of companionship with God.

It is an image of the Christian life not primarily as believing or being good but as a relationship with God. That relationship does not leave us unchanged but transforms us into more and more compassionate beings, "into the likeness of Christ." It is the vision of the Christian life spoken of so eloquently by Paul in a densely packed passage in 2 Corinthians:

> And we all, with unveiled faces, beholding the glory of the Lord, are being transformed into the likeness of Christ from one degree of glory to another. And this comes from the Lord, the Spirit.[31]

Beholding the Spirit, we are being changed into the likeness of Christ.

I want to close by talking about a very familiar Christian phrase—*believing in Jesus*—and how it is related to the image of the Christian life that has emerged in this book. For those of us who grew up in the church, believing in Jesus was important. For me, what that phrase used to mean, in my childhood and into my early adulthood, was "believing things about Jesus." To believe in Jesus meant to believe what the gospels and the church said about Jesus. That was easy when I was a child, and became more and more difficult as I grew older.

But I now see that believing in Jesus can (and does) mean something very different from that. The change is pointed to by the root meaning of the word *believe*. *Believe* did not originally mean believing a set of doctrines or teachings; in both Greek and Latin its roots mean "to give one's heart to."[32] The "heart" is the self at its deepest level. *Believing*, therefore, does not consist of giving one's mental assent to something, but involves a much deeper level of one's self. Believing in Jesus does not mean believing doctrines about him. Rather, it means to give one's heart, one's self at its deepest level, to the post-Easter Jesus who is the living Lord, the side of God turned toward us, the face of God, the Lord who is also the Spirit.

Believing in Jesus in the sense of giving one's heart to Jesus is the movement from secondhand religion to firsthand religion, from having heard about Jesus with the hearing of the ear to being in relationship with the Spirit of Christ. For ultimately, Jesus is not simply a figure of the past, but a figure of the present. Meeting that Jesus—the living Jesus who comes to us even now—will be like meeting Jesus again for the first time.

NOTES

1. A book often cited as foundational for this movement is Hans Frei, *The Eclipse of Biblical Narrative: A Study in Eighteenth and Nineteenth Century Hermeneutics* (New Haven, CT: Yale Univ. Press, 1974). Story theology became widely known through John Shea's popular-level book *Stories of God* (Chicago: Thomas More Press, 1978). See also William J. Bausch, *Story-Telling: Imagination and Faith* (Mystic, CT: Twenty-Third Publications, 1984); and Terrence W. Tilley, *Story Theology* (Wilmington, DE: Michael Glazier, 1985).

2. This is a subject on which I have recently been working and which I hope soon to develop into a book, tentatively titled *Scripture, Story, and the Christian Journey.*

3. I am not irrevocably committed to there being three and only three macro-stories. Despite the Trinity, there is nothing sacred about the number three. Thus I am open to one or more additional stories being identified as macro-stories. Serious candidates would include stories of blindness and seeing (and the related theme of darkness

and light) and stories of sickness and healing. However, important as these are, they do not seem to me as central as the three stories I will highlight.

4. William James, *The Varieties of Religious Experience,* ed. Martin Marty (New York: Penguin, 1982; originally published in 1902), p. 508.

5. Walter Brueggemann, *The Bible Makes Sense* (Atlanta: John Knox, 1977), especially chap. 3. On pp. 45–46, Brueggemann speaks of Israel's primal narrative as "that most simple, elemental, and non-negotiable story line which lies at the heart of biblical faith. . . . It is an affirmation in story form which asserts, 'This is the most important story we know, and we have come to believe it is decisively about us.'"

6. Deut. 6.21–23. This passage and Deut. 26.5–9 are seen by scholars as very ancient pieces of oral tradition, much older than the document in which they appear, and as the core of the fuller story told by the Pentateuch as a whole. They have been called Israel's most ancient "confessions of faith."

7. Maurice Samuel, trans., *Haggadah of Passover* (New York: Hebrew Publishing, 1942), p. 27. Italics added; translation slightly modified for the sake of using gender-inclusive language.

8. The phrases are from Walter Brueggemann, *The Prophetic Imagination* (Philadelphia: Fortress, 1978), chap. 2.

9. For biblical descriptions of the experience of exile, see especially Isaiah 40–55 (a portion of the book of Isaiah commonly referred to as "Second Isaiah" or "Deutero-Isaiah"). Though these chapters ring out with the good news of return, they also contain moving descriptions of what life in exile is like. See also Psalm 137, a psalm of exile; and the book of Lamentations, which describes the suffering, despair, and angst of the generation living after the destruction of Jerusalem and the temple.

10. See, for example, James Sanders, *Torah and Canon* (Philadelphia: Fortress, 1972); Sanders emphasizes that much of the Hebrew Bible came into existence during and immediately after the exile, when the first of its three parts, the Pentateuch or Torah, was put into its final form, and the second of its three parts, the prophets, began to take shape. Broadening his scope to include the New Testament as well, Sanders provocatively and correctly comments, on p. 6: "The Bible comes to us out of the ashes of two Temples, the Solomonic Temple, destroyed in 586 B.C., and the Herodian Temple, destroyed in A.D. 70."

11. Psalms 137.1. The experience of exile can also generate intense anger, which is expressed in the closing verses of this psalm.

12. Isaiah 40.3–4. The beautiful and powerful language of this prophet has become very familiar through its widespread use in Handel's *Messiah*.

13. Interestingly, the Hebrew word that we translate as "repent" originally meant "return," and thus has its linguistic home within the story of exile and return.

14. Isaiah 40.29–31. Other examples of the language of return: Isaiah 40.11, 42.16, 43.1–21, 48.20–21, 49.8–12, 51.9–11.

15. To avoid a possible misunderstanding, by "priestly story" I do not mean the "priestly" or "P" source of the Pentateuch (even though regulations for the priesthood and sacrifice are a major theme of that source). Rather, I mean a way of imaging the religious life that sees it as a story of sin, guilt, sacrifice, and forgiveness.

16. Paul Ricoeur, *The Symbolism of Evil*, trans. Emerson Buchanan (Boston: Beacon, 1967).

17. Gustaf Aulen, *Christus Victor*, trans. A. G. Hebert (New York: Macmillan, 1969; originally published in 1931). Aulen later became a bishop of the Church of Sweden (Lutheran).

18. Aulen, in *Christus Victor*, argues that this understanding was first systematically developed by Anselm, archbishop of Canterbury, in a work entitled *Cur Deus Homo?*, dated to 1097.

19. Aulen, in *Christus Victor*, calls the third understanding the "subjective" or "moral exemplar" theory of the atonement. To me, he seems much less interested in this understanding than he is in the contrasts between the first two, and his exposition of the third type of understanding strikes me as less satisfactory and appreciative. I thus depart somewhat from his argument at this point.

20. John 3.16.

21. Because the following indictment of the priestly story is severe, I wish to add a couple of clarifying remarks. First, the indictment is of the *popular understanding* of the priestly story. There is a more theologically sophisticated understanding of it that underlines its truly radical quality, to which I will briefly refer later. Second, the indictment is of the priestly story when it stands alone as the primary way of imaging the Christian life. As I point out later in this chapter, when the priestly story is seen in the context of the journey story of which it is a part, its limitations are overcome.

22. See Exodus 25–40, where the regulations for priests and sacrifices are given in the wilderness.

23. It is striking that Mark, the earliest gospel, emphasizes "way" imagery so much. One of Mark's favorite words is *hodos*, which may be translated as "road," "path," or "way." Mark opens his gospel with the passage from 2 Isaiah about a "way in the wilderness," and the Jesus of Mark teaches repeatedly about "the way," especially in the central section (Mark 8–10) when he begins his journey to Jerusalem and death. So also in the gospel of Luke: at the center is a journey narrative (Luke 9.51–18.14). And in Acts, the author of Luke-Acts reports that the earliest name of the Christian movement was "the Way" (Acts 9.2).

24. Though I have not done a thorough study yet, my hunch is that most or all of the New Testament references to the death of Jesus as being in some sense a sacrifice can be understood in this subversive way.

25. There is an unfortunate irony here. In the documents that became the New Testament, imaging the death of Jesus as a sacrifice for sin originally subverted the priestly story; but when the New Testament became sacred Scripture, these same texts *established* the priestly story as the central Christian story. As a consequence the emphasis changed from seeing the story of Jesus-as-sacrifice as *undermining* the priestly story to *believing* in the priestly story (with Jesus now as the central figure in the story).

26. I am using "disciples," as the gospels themselves do, as a broader category than simply "the twelve apostles."

27. Edward Schillebeeckx, *Jesus* (New York: Crossroad, 1981), p. 201.

28. Discipleship involves having *companions*, a word that means "someone with whom one shares bread."

29. Shea, *Stories of God*, p. 8.

30. See chapter 1 of this book, pp. 2–3.

31. 2 Corinthians 3.18.

32. Wilfred Cantwell Smith, *Faith and Belief* (Princeton, NJ: Princeton Univ. Press, 1979), pp. 76–78. One can see this also in the German word *belieben*, which is the immediate root of the English word *believe*. *Belieben* does not mean "to believe," but rather "to belove." Thus *to believe* is more properly understood as "to belove." See Smith's discussion on pp. 105–27.

Index